"At Weston's inaugural Juneteenth celebration, the vibrant atmosphere created a sense of unity and it became clear that this celebration was more than just a commemoration; it was a catalyst for dialogue about history and progress and fostered a deeper understanding of the significance of freedom and equality."
—**Samantha Nestor, First Selectwoman, Town of Weston**

"An intriguing, compelling, ambitious and well-researched book that gives insight into a world most of us have not encountered. Daniels and Wiesen go to remarkable depths to tell Harriet Tubman's true story. It resonated with me to such profound levels that it sometimes moved me to tears."
—**Anni Domingo, author of *Breaking the Maafa Chain***

"As the first African American Selectman of Weston, it was with great pride that the keynote speaker on Junteenth was Rita Daniels, whose account enlightened the audience with her intellectual honesty and captivating delivery. Jean Marie Wiesen's extensive research, coupled with Rita's riveting testimonies, give a different perspective and deeper insight into my hero, the fierce Harriet Tubman."
—**Martin Mohabeer, Former Selectman, Town of Weston**

"I had the distinct pleasure of personally meeting Rita Daniels, the great-great-great-grandniece of Harriet Tubman. I listened intently while she elaborated on oral history passed down through the generations, telling the rich story of one of America's most beloved iconic figures. At last, she and Jean Marie Wiesen have put these stories on paper, filling in numerous gaps and correcting many longstanding errors. This book should be read by every American."
—**Richard Blumenthal, United States Senator, State of Connecticut**

"In *Harriet Tubman*, familiar aspects of Tubman's story are accentuated and expanded with what has been gleaned from family lore. Character traits and sensibilities, like Tubman's famed curative skills as an herbalist, are placed within a powerful context and linked to a family's African roots and her descendants' ongoing work. Having had a front-row seat to the ways Tubman has been studied, dissected, and honored, Daniels grants both authoritative history and authentic humanity to a story frequently segmented for political expediency or specialized study, leaving readers with a fuller understanding of Tubman's unique bravery, fortitude, and leadership."
—*Kirkus Reviews*

HARRIET TUBMAN

MILITARY SCOUT AND TENACIOUS VISIONARY

From Her Roots in Ghana to Her Legacy on the Eastern Shore

Jean Marie Wiesen and Rita Daniels,

Great-great-great-grandniece of Harriet Tubman

FOREWORD BY QUEEN MOTHER DR. DELOIS BLAKELY

PEGASUS BOOKS

NEW YORK LONDON

HARRIET TUBMAN

Pegasus Books, Ltd.
148 West 37th Street, 13th Floor
New York, NY 10018

Copyright © 2025 by Jean Marie Wiesen and Rita Daniels

Foreword copyright © 2025 by Queen Mother Dr. Delois Blakely

First Pegasus Books cloth edition February 2025

Interior design by Maria Fernandez

This publication is presented solely for informational, educational, and
entertainment purposes. Any oversights or inaccuracies are unintentional.

Library of Congress Cataloging-in-Publication Data is available.

ISBN: 978-1-63936-813-6

10 9 8 7 6 5 4 3 2 1

Printed in the United States of America
Distributed by Simon & Schuster
www.pegasusbooks.com

After escaping the severe beatings and humiliation of slavery, Harriet Tubman made it her mission to help others seek freedom. Throughout her life, Tubman faced many struggles but persisted in her fight for justice. She fought for enslaved people, served in the Union Army during the Civil War, and advocated for women's rights. She proudly boasted, "I was the conductor of the Underground Railroad for eight years, and I can say what most conductors can't say—I never ran my train off the track, and I never lost a passenger."

—Rita Daniels and Pauline Copes Johnson

To thine own self be true . . .

—Jean Marie Wiesen, with gratitude to
Shakespeare's Polonius (in *Hamlet*)

My Uncle Don stood by me every step of the way on this project from its inception in June of 2022 until his passing in November of 2023. If it had not been for his loving encouragement, guidance, and nearly daily phone calls, I don't know if this book would have been completed—he's always been my champion with grace and humor. A week before his passing, he promised he would always watch over me, and I believe he is.

—Jean

I hold dear to me the memory of my mother, Geraldine Copes Daniels, who passed away in March 2020. Her unwavering support and belief in me drove my pursuit of an MBA in Education and the establishment of the Harriet Tubman Learning Center (HTLC). She firmly believed that the HTLC was not just a tribute but a crucial institution in perpetuating the legacy of our Aunt Harriet Tubman. As a formerly enslaved person, Harriet Tubman was denied a formal education, making the establishment of the Learning Center a significant step in honoring our Aunt's legacy.

—Rita

CONTENTS

Queen Mother Dr. Delois Blakely in front of the
Harriet Tubman statue in Harlem, New York.

FOREWORD

E ducation of the underserved has been my passion for as long as I can recall—assisting those in the direst need among us. I was honored to be appointed United Nations Goodwill Ambassador to numerous African Nations, including Ghana, several decades ago, which was a high honor for me. My being named Community Mayor of Harlem is an equal honor, as well. When I was approached to write the foreword for *Harriet Tubman:*

Military Scout and Tenacious Visionary, I did not hesitate. The phrase, "Ain't I a woman," spoken by Sojourner Truth, a close ally of Harriet Tubman's, came to mind. We're all of a similar background, with the same mission—freeing those who are in bondage. Too many stories abound of Harriet Tubman, none of which an author has penned directly with a descendant of Harriet's since Sarah Bradford Hopkins herself interviewed Harriet in 1886. Finally, Jean Marie Wiesen, an investigative author, has carefully researched and collaborated with Rita Daniels, a three-time-great-grand-niece of Harriet Tubman. We learn more of Harriet's immense courage, spirit, and leadership skills under fire in spite of a childhood head trauma. Harriet's theme throughout her life was putting others first until her final breath.

Come on, come on, come on through! Like a river.
—Queen Mother Dr. Delois Blakely

PREFACE

by Rita Daniels

G rowing up in Auburn, New York, I was always inquisitive. I will never forget some of the stories passed on to me and my siblings. The most fascinating story to me was about being related to an enslaved woman who also lived in Auburn, New York, for fifty-plus years. This woman happened to be Harriet Tubman. I wasn't sure if I should be happy or not when I was informed that I was related to this enslaved woman. One must understand that the only stories about her that were read in our history books back in the day were about one to two paragraphs long and described her as a fugitive with a bounty on her head. I remember in the third grade; I was given a task to write about this enslaved woman, not knowing that I was going to be shocked to find out that I was related to her. What! I was about to lose my mind; how in the world am I related to this woman?

I remember speaking to several other relatives who informed me of the great deeds this woman, Harriet Tubman, had done in all her years. I visited the property where the Home for the Aged is, and her home in Auburn. I became even more fascinated when I discovered that the history books were wrong about Harriet Tubman by omitting most of the crucial information regarding her life leading up to the Combahee River Raid and beyond. Her life was more heroic than what was illustrated in history books, either back then or today. We now understand that Sarah Bradford Hopkins was unable to complete her entire interview with Harriet because of Harriet's declining health. Harriet focused on saving her people, regardless of what she might personally lose in the process—before the Civil War and afterward. She advocated for equal voting rights long before it became fashionable—an often overlooked fact. This is precisely why we wrote this book: to fill in the gaps and correct inaccuracies.

My mother, Geraldine Copes Daniels, and I started the Harriet Tubman Learning Center in 2016 to ensure that the legacy of Harriet Tubman continues through education, regardless of a person's ability to pay. The Center relies solely on donations as a 501c nonprofit organization. Harriet Tubman was not able to obtain an education as an enslaved person because it was against the law during that era. You can visit our website at https://www.harriettubmanlearningcenter.org if you would like to learn more about what the Learning Center offers.

Harriet Tubman freed enslaved people and took them through the Underground Railroad, becoming the Moses of her people (just like the Moses in the Bible). Harriet survived and served in the military during the Civil War; she became a nurse and healer to the injured soldiers and an advocate for the women's suffragists. Even though she was denied an education and could not read, she could still promote education. Harriet Tubman's legacy will not be forgotten because of the many statues sculpted and placed in various locations in her honor over the years and throughout the world, including Ghana and Canada.

Harriet Tubman became our reason to be free because of her journey and fight for freedom! We need to segue from her story to what we are doing today to continue the legacy of Harriet Tubman: What are we doing now? The Harriet Tubman Learning Center must keep the legacy and heritage to honor her fight for freedom through education because she could not read or write! She deserves it, and we deserve reparations, perhaps through further education—college or trade school of the individual's choosing. My great-great-great-aunt Harriet remained illiterate her entire life, and I believe that regardless of the career path one chooses, one must be able to read and write. For example, construction workers must be able to read instructions and write notes detailing the tasks that need to be carried out. It's one of the reasons my mother and I felt so strongly about opening the Harriet Tubman Learning Center: to continue Harriet's legacy of "keep going in the face of adversity." We will never know the people from our past and how they survived from generation to generation. But if we do not understand our past, how do we ensure people won't repeat the same mistakes? We cannot disappoint our ancestors. We must keep going and make a difference.

Our ancestors faced challenge after challenge, which eventually presented opportunities for change, which we live through today. For example, they marched in Birmingham, were hosed in Selma, were assassinated in Memphis, were segregated in the South, and were relegated to ghettoes in the North. These historical events became the pivotal resurrection points for our ancestors' fight for freedom. For some reason, their stories are ignored in history books, and they are stereotyped in Hollywood.

We will never understand the exact pain endured and how hard our ancestors had to work for their survival. Still, we do know that because our ancestors were mistreated, we are working to ensure that we do not let their sacrifices be forgotten. We do this by ensuring that the present and the future do not repeat what our ancestors had to live through. Working together is the only way we can right the wrongs of the past.

Each year, our families would visit the Harriet Tubman Home for the Aged for a family reunion and stay on the property. We would stay in our motor homes, RVs, tents, etc., and enjoy a lovely long weekend where we had cookouts, fashion shows, storytelling, and many games. These family reunions were celebrated each year until they were no longer allowed once it became a national park.

HARRIET TUBMAN

1

HERITAGE

To understand who Harriet Tubman was, one needs to know her roots and acknowledge her Ashanti tribal heritage in Accra, central coastal Ghana. But she was born far from Accra. Harriet's story begins on Maryland's Eastern Shore. Born Araminta, she was the fifth of nine children of Harriet Green (whose nickname was Rit) and Ben Ross. Rit and Ben's known children were Linah (1808), Mariah (also known as Mary, 1811), Sophe (1813), Robert (1816–1893), Araminta (Minty, March 1822–March 10, 1913), Ben (1823), Rachel (1825–1859), Henry (1830), and Moses (1832). Death dates are not known for all of Harriet's siblings, as some were sold into slavery and never seen again by Harriet.

The name Araminta means prayer and protection and is of Hebrew origin. Her parents lovingly referred to her as Minty. Although slave birth records were not maintained, it has been estimated Minty was born sometime in March of 1822 on the Anthony Thompson farm in Peter's Neck, Dorchester County, Maryland. Araminta's mother, Rit, was the "property" of Mary Pattison Brodess, who had inherited enslaved people from her late grandfather, Atthow Pattison. However, uncertainty remains to this day regarding the exact year. It is known that Minty's maternal grandmother, Modesty, a name given to her by her future slave master, was born in Accra, Ghana, and was captured and stolen from her family when she was in her late teens. According to family history, Modesty was then sold as an enslaved person. It is known that she was part of the Ashanti tribe, but there are no records of her birth parents or the year she was forced to make the voyage aboard a slave ship to Maryland. There are no records of what happened to her family members. There are several references to Modesty in other historical works and, according to family lore, Modesty did not meet her granddaughter, Minty, until several moments before her passing.

The Ashanti, also known as Asante, were undoubtedly the largest tribe in Ghana and were part of the Akan ethnic group. They migrated to the rainforest areas along the Atlantic shoreline after the fall of the Old Ghana Empire in the thirteenth century. It is well documented that they discovered an incredibly vast amount of gold ore in this area, which gave them enormous wealth and bargaining power until the eighteenth century. The Ashanti grew yams, cocoa, vegetables, legumes, maize, plantains, and onions in the fertile soil of the coast, which made up their starchy and vegetable diet. They are world renowned for their wood carvings and colorful Kente weavings, which date back centuries.

In the Ashanti civilization, the family, including the extended family, is of the utmost importance. The Ashanti are a matrilineal society, with the mother's clan being the most revered. According to their beliefs, a child is said to receive flesh and blood from the mother and inherit the soul or spirit from the father. The family remains close by, even in a nuclear fashion, as they grow up, marry, and move into their own homes or huts. Marriage is integral to their culture; however, women will not marry without the consent of their parents. Divorce is extremely rare among Ashanti. If necessary, the parents take it upon themselves to intervene to keep a marriage on track.

The Ashanti's cultural philosophy combines spiritual and supernatural powers. They firmly believe that plants and animals have souls and, as a result, deserve the utmost respect. They acknowledge the healing powers of many plants and herbs and consider themselves the ultimate physicians of natural medicine through what nature has provided. This practice is orally taught and passed down through the generations, and it manifested in Minty's own herbal medicinal mastery, which was taught to her by her mother and father. Modesty's Ghanaian roots and the endurance of Ashanti oral cultural traditions were still on full display in her granddaughter's knowledge and that of others in their community.

The Akan language, spoken by the Ashanti and brought with them across the Middle Passage, has links to ancient biblical writings. Today, many Ghanaians give their children names resembling those in the Bible. The first account of the Akans appears in the book of Genesis, chapter 36, verses 26–27, and states they are of Horite descent. These groups played an essential role in the biblical documentation of the scriptures. Several names, like Noah, Amos, and Joseph, were frequently used in biblical literature. Akan naming traditions include giving many of the same names to their children, such as Boah, Amoh, and Benefo. As a result of these accounts, many believe the Akan had a hand in writing the Bible and the Torah.

By the early nineteenth century, the Ashanti had begun to fight several wars with Britain. Their territory covered most of modern Ghana, and they traded directly with the British. They maintained their wealth in gold, allowing them to wield power over potential enemies. They enslaved people they captured from warring tribes and sold both gold and enslaved people to Europeans, the American Colonies, and the British in exchange for guns.

Before enslaved people were even boarded, they were stripped of all their clothing and put in chains. The slave ships were typically filled beyond capacity on their fateful journeys to the American Colonies. Subsequently, there was a low survival rate due to disease, close quarters below decks, unsanitary conditions, deliberate starvation, and lack of clean drinking water.

There were enough survivors despite the disease-ridden conditions aboard the ship and, fortunately, Minty's grandmother, Modesty, was among them. Minty's father, Ben, also had Ashanti roots and taught her celestial navigation and which healing roots were safe to gather in the Dorchester woods. These teachings could have come from both sides of the family, having their origins in the Ashanti tribe. It's fascinating to note that many roots and healing plants found in Ghana, the ancestral home of the Ashanti, are also found in Dorchester, Maryland, and its surrounding areas, creating a geographical connection between the two.

The Ashanti, a tribe steeped in rich cultural practices, are renowned for their singing and drumming during ceremonies such as births, marriages, funerals, and important announcements. The drumming, a powerful precursor to these ceremonies, serves as a call for villagers to gather, resonating far and wide. This drumming, a code understood by the villagers, is reminiscent of the singing Harriet Tubman would later employ to announce her secret arrival to the still-captive enslaved people. The familiarity of the ancestral words sung and the drumming beat served as a signal to the enslaved, who instinctively knew to trust that Harriet had arrived.

2

CASTLES OF TORMENT

Numerous exotic castles dot the southern coast of Ghana, overlooking the Gulf of Guinea, which connects with the Atlantic Ocean to the east. Two of the more famous of these are the Elmina and the Cape Coast Castles. The Elmina (St. George's Castle) was built in 1482 by the Portuguese, who later built the Cape Coast, in 1555, as a trade lodge. This portion of the Ghanaian coast had already become known as the Gold Coast because of the massive amounts of gold discovered by explorers. The castles were built as fortifications against other Europeans, who might attack and steal the gold, as well as against warring tribal Africans, whose wealth was being stolen from beneath them. The Portuguese were the first settlers of the Gold Coast, but their forts were eventually attacked, overwhelmed, seized by Spaniards, and sold, during several centuries of struggles among European powers competing over control of the Gold Coast. African tribal factions were caught in the middle while watching their most valuable commodities, gold and ivory, depart their shores. These tribes spent the next several centuries at war with each other and with the Europeans, as they sought to regain some control over their gold and wealth, which was disappearing from their shores almost daily.

Elmina Castle in Ghana

Later in the 1500s, another demand came on the radar: human trading, as increased domestic and agricultural labor became primary requirements in the British Empire and the Caribbean. The castles turned from storage facilities for gold and ivory to holding areas for human beings as they awaited transport to points east via as many ships as possible.

The transnational transaction of slavery went on well into the 1700s and 1800s until it was finally abolished worldwide; it was outlawed in the United States in 1807. The slave trade flourished in the South and remained legal in some midwestern states and the West as well as throughout much of Europe and the West Indies. During those years, the numbers varied from twelve million to as high as fifteen million African men, women, and children who were enslaved and transported to the Americas, making it the most significant forced long-distance movement of people in recorded history. It is also estimated that 10–19 percent of those millions perished on the Middle Passage voyage across the Atlantic due to the horrid conditions aboard the ships. Most of the enslaved people bound for the Colonies came from West Africa. Ghanaians also sold their own people, without hesitation, to the Europeans. One of those people was Modesty, the grandmother of Harriet Tubman.

3

FROM ONE HELL
TO ANOTHER

Following their capture by rival Ghanaian tribes, prisoners like Modesty were taken to what is now referred to as "The Slave River"—or its Ghanaian name, Donkor Nsuo—for a final cleansing, or bath, before being taken to either of the two castles, just over twenty-four miles to the east down a winding, dusty road under the hot sun. Most captives were without footwear as they walked along the road in chains. It was the final walk in their homeland before being sold, primarily to European and Euro-American slaveholders.

The slave trade was conducted by the Portuguese and the Dutch in the 1600s, and they were known to auction off their captives in the castle courtyards before these souls were chained again and taken below to the dungeons. There were separate dungeons for men and women, where they might spend several months waiting for ships to take them to their ultimate destinations. Nothing changed as the calendar rolled to the next century other than the faces of the desperate men, women, and children, many of whom died before ever boarding the ships. In the eighteenth century, the courtyard was called "the great depot."

Photographs of the Female Slave Dungeons at Elmina Castle

Photographs of the Male Slave Dungeons at Elmina Castle

Meager food scraps were tossed to them; some chose to eat, while others preferred to die. Those who did die were thrown into the sea. In the dungeons, the only ventilation was one small porthole, giving the captives nothing to counteract the stench they were forced to live with for weeks. Everything that flowed from their bodies emptied into a central dip in the middle of the dungeon and made its way out into the sea. The cells the enslaved people were forced into held up to several hundred at a time, not leaving enough room for anyone to lie down. Sanitation was of no concern to the enslavers, making outbreaks of disease common.

In stark contrast, above these squalid dungeons were suites extravagantly decorated with the latest in European design for those who engaged in the prosperous transatlantic slave trade. While the enslaved people below them starved and suffered—and many perished—the passengers staying in the suites dined on whatever they desired.

When it was time for the enslaved to leave the castle and board the ships, they were chained once again and led through what is now referred to as the Door of No Return. They had to crouch to pass through, their bare feet on the filthy stone as they made their way in the dark until the first bit of sunlight they had seen since they had been imprisoned hit them, and they breathed in fresh air for the first time in weeks. They stared at the angry sea crashing against the rocks below, taking note of the numerous ships lined up, bobbing in the water. They wondered if that was where they were going and how they would get down there. The guards shoved them toward a pulley that lowered them individually onto the decks of the waiting ships until the ships were filled with their human cargo and ready to undertake the transatlantic voyage. Once they were below deck, the vessel set sail easterly for the Atlantic Ocean.

Modesty was one of approximately 12.5 million enslaved Africans who survived the transatlantic voyage to the Americas between 1500 and 1866, the year the Civil Rights Act ended slavery as a legal institution in the United States. Roughly 1.8 million of her African brothers and sisters would die on the journey for a variety of reasons—suicide, disease, beatings, and other causes—while onboard.

Photographs of the Door of No Return at Elmina Castle

The size of a slave ship determined the number of crew and the amount of cargo she could carry from port to port. Some ships could carry a crew of up to one hundred and as many as seven hundred enslaved individuals below deck.

Men and women were kept in separate compartments. The men were always chained and shackled in pairs, whereas the women remained unchained, yet they were confined in equally cramped spaces. Children might have the run of the ship, depending on the boat and the captain. Neither the men, the children, nor the women had much airflow, like the conditions of the dungeons they had recently left behind. Again, the conditions were extremely unsanitary, leading to all sorts of diseases, including dysentery and smallpox, coupled with sexual exploitation at the hands of the captain and the crew. The crew regularly whipped the enslaved people, some of whom revolted by refusing to eat the few scraps they were given. In contrast, others jumped overboard when they had the opportunity.

Like in the dungeons, where the enslaved people were cramped into cells and their European captors dined sumptuously, the captain and his officers lived in comparative luxury. They had their own cabin space, usually below the raised quarterdeck at the ship's stern. The regular crew slept on the main deck beneath a protective tarp or in a longboat that would be used for the crew's escape should the boat sink. No thought was given to the people in chains beneath the floorboards.

Initially, the ships were general merchant vessels. Then, as time passed, adjustments were made to keep the wooden boats from rotting. Merchants discovered that using copper-sheathed hulls kept the wood from rotting and the boring worms found in tropical waters at bay. Now and then, the ships were modified to increase the size and number of portholes below deck, increasing the airflow to slow the spread of disease. Even with these modifications, the disease made its way from below deck to the crew above, and many were lost during the voyages across the Atlantic. With the changes aboard the ships, the mortality rate for both the enslaved people and the ship's crew went from roughly 20 percent during the first decades of slave trading to approximately 10 percent by the 1800s. These improvements more than likely increased Modesty's chances of survival.

Other necessary changes included adding muskets, cannons, and swivel guns to the upper deck to ward off pirate attacks when sailing from France to coastal Africa to collect their human cargo during the mid to late 1700s.

It was not only the enslaved who committed suicide by jumping over-board; it was occasionally some of the crew because of the harsh treatment by the officers combined with contagious diseases. The dead were tossed overboard with no regard. Sharks were known to follow the ships through the warm waters.

One could equate the captain of a slave ship to a plantation owner—he expected his orders to be followed without question. Several of the crew had been forced to work for shipping companies due to personal debts or run-ins with the law, putting them at the captain's mercy. Crew members habitually took out their rage on the enslaved.

When he first came ashore, the captain would have sold his cargo, con-sisting of arms, tools, and cloth, on the Gold Coast in exchange for humans housed in the castles, and then transported his new cargo to the Americas. These people would then be sold at auction, with money going to the ship's owners. A share of the funds went to the captain, giving him a vested interest in maintaining complete control of his crew and human cargo. If there was a danger of disease becoming rampant among the enslaved, the captain would order the crew to throw living enslaved people overboard to control the further spread of disease. The ship's insurance company covered these losses.

The captain would have ordered the crew to separate the enslaved, separating not only men and women but also families, friends, and people who spoke the same language. Even though their prisoners were shackled and chained, the captain wanted to minimize the potential of revolt. But enslaved people who spoke different languages managed to find ways to communicate with each other, using sign language. They sang their tribal songs to lift their spirits as best they could.

At the end of a Middle Passage voyage, those who had survived had developed friendships through all they had endured, only to be separated again. They were cleaned with palm oil to improve their appearance at auction, either onboard or at a market onshore. Once sold, they would be given English names, in a further effort to erase their identities and heritage.

4

MODESTY SURVIVES THE ATLANTIC OCEAN VOYAGE

An Ashanti maiden named Modesty was born in Ghana, on the Gold Coast of Africa. She was among the hundreds of West Africans captured from her village in the late 1700s. She was part of the Ashanti tribe, uprooted from her home in the Kumasi Region of Africa. Once the slave traders captured all the younger men and women, the people left behind were the unwanted elders and young children.

Modesty was one of several hundred in bondage heading to Elmina Castle along the Gulf of Guinea. The enslaved reached a camp in Assin Praso, where they were tortured, shackled, and whipped by the slave traders to show they were no longer in control. Modesty would not allow someone to torture her without fighting back; however, she was powerless with the chains and shackles holding her down. The only thing Modesty could think of was whether her family was alive or dead. She wondered what had happened to her village and whether she would ever return home.

Modesty dragged her blood-covered body along the slave route, a dusty road they had been forced to walk beneath the blazing hot Ghanaian sun. Sweat had probably streaked down Modesty's back, which was covered with dust that had been kicked up by her bare feet. The slave traders had taken their shoes and any jewelry or fancy clothing they had been wearing. They were left wearing the bare minimum, which may have been in tatters after hours of forced walking each day, rubbing against sweaty, chafed, and bloody skin and chains.

After weeks of walking, the enslaved people were escorted in small groups into the Manso River to wash off their bloodstained, sweaty bodies. The blood had hardened because of the hot sun gleaming directly on them, so this was a welcomed cleansing. Afterward, the slave traders gave them red palm oil to soften the dryness of their skin. From there, their bodies were examined (i.e., teeth, ears, eyes, feet, and hands), only to be branded with extremely hot irons to indicate ownership. Some of the enslaved were left behind because they were not fit to go any farther; they had become ill as they journeyed by foot, still in chains and shackles, to their next destination.

The only thoughts of the slave traders were of the money, gold, guns, and jewelry they would receive once they delivered their cargo to their final destinations. These slave traders were headed to the dungeons of Elmina Castle to await the ships that would transport the survivors.

Modesty, still chained but able to continue walking, could see the ocean's waves breaking against the rocky shore. On her other side, she saw the enormous white castle with many cannons pointed toward the sea. After being kidnapped from her family, chained, and forced to walk for days, Modesty might have wondered if her fortune was about to change. Was this where she would be living? She had many questions but was too afraid to ask them.

As they approached the castle, it became apparent that the men and women would be separated; there was a female dungeon and a male dungeon. Modesty and around two hundred other women entered the female dungeon. The male dungeon would hold twice as many. Neither dungeon was better than the other; they were both dark and dingy and smelled foul. From there, they awaited the ships that would transport them across the Atlantic Ocean to a new world, the land of the unknown.

In these dungeons there was no personal space for the captured and soon-to-be enslaved. They were crammed into these death camps with little concern for their health, emotions, or physical well-being.

Modesty, the daughter of a powerful warrior, was one of the many strong females who managed to survive capture and abuse. Her determination demonstrated the strength she would pass on to her descendants.

The torture was relentless. Every evening, she and several other women were washed and fed. This was so they would be presentable before being paraded to the courtyard to satisfy the sexual demands of the governor.

It seemed like the dungeon doors would never open, but they finally did. The overseers led the men and women through the gateway exit known as the Door of No Return. Still shackled to one another by their hands, legs, and necks, they could finally inhale fresh ocean air. Still, they were treated like nothing more than cargo as they were loaded onto small boats.

The horrors of the Middle Passage were about to begin, and the passengers had no idea what to expect. What could be worse than the inhumane journey they had encountered on the path to the dungeons? Now they were packed like sardines into these small boats, heading to a ship with White men who didn't look anything like them. They could not understand the language the White men spoke, either.

The arduous journey was another unexpected horror for Modesty, taking over fifty days. She displayed enormous strength and survival skills while holding back her tears of fear. The men and women—who were chained separately and on opposite sides of the ship—were connected side by side with no room to move around or breathe. They were treated worse than animals, and the smell of sweat, urine, feces, blood, vomit, and dead bodies always surrounded them. Some of those who didn't survive were thrown overboard, while others remained chained to the living, causing them additional hardships. Some chained captives jumped into the sea with the corpses, willing to end their lives rather than continue their misery. Modesty remained focused and stayed the course, knowing that the ship had to land somewhere at some point.

The boat finally stopped, docking at the Eastern Shore of Maryland. At first, it was a welcome relief. Modesty hoped this was where she would be rescued, and her nightmare would finally end. But it didn't. The now enslaved "gold" was unloaded from the boat: lightly clothed, scared, dirty, and smelly. Their chains were removed so they could be rubbed down with red palm oil once again before being escorted to the marketplace to be auctioned off. She was frightened, as she was aware that the White men were sizing her up to purchase her. Once the captives were lined up, Modesty was among the first to be sold. A White man named John Green offered the highest bid. According to the auctioneer, Modesty was controllable, relatively healthy, and strong. She was one of the six million Africans transported to North America between 1700 and 1800.

5

JOHN GREEN

John Green was a well-to-do tobacco planter from Dorchester County. As far as he was concerned, his newly purchased young enslaved woman was a desirable prize. He was especially keen on her performing chores that would make life for his wife, Prudence, far more manageable. While Mr. Green drank his brandy, he named his newly acquired prized possession Modesty. Her Ashanti name has since been forever lost.

Green already had another enslaved person, Sarah, to serve as a house worker, but he felt she was getting on in years and assigned her to train Modesty as her replacement. Modesty was determined to do her best by learning the ropes and the newly acquired English language, which she knew would be essential for survival.

The woman who looked like she belonged to her tribe accepted Modesty and helped her adjust. She learned how to act in the Big House and knew her place. She could understand the language, but as time passed, she felt that the master had his eyes on her, making her uncomfortable.

Master Green was beginning to think about what he would do to Modesty if only he could have her to himself. He began to visualize encountering Modesty and knew this day would soon come. That day came! Modesty had to let herself go and not fight the master's demands during these many encounters. As far as Modesty was concerned, she had no choice but to please her master.

In enslaved and enslaver situations, the truth is difficult to hear and comprehend. Enslavers had complete control at every turn, whereas the enslaved had none; they were physical property. To survive, they had to follow their master's every command, regardless of their wishes. This included whatever their master's desires might be at any given moment. Many children born on southern plantations and farms resulted from enslavers taking advantage of enslaved women whenever they felt the impulse. Enslaved women had little choice but to set their feelings aside and acquiesce.

One morning, Modesty woke up sick to her stomach. She had no idea what was happening to her body, but she still went to work. The enslaved people knew that sickness was not a reason to stay away from work. While Modesty was doing her chores, she felt very nauseated and, this time, she had the urge to throw up. Modesty ran out of the house and vomited. One of the other enslaved workers saw what was going on; she told Modesty that she was with child. Modesty felt surprised and relieved now that she understood what was happening to her body.

As months passed and Modesty's belly grew more prominent, it was apparent that her pregnancy was no secret to anyone, including Master Green. When Modesty began feeling very sharp labor pains, two other enslaved women helped her prepare for the birth. It came within minutes, and the baby cried. Modesty had just given birth to her daughter Henrietta. Little did she know her beautiful daughter would eventually give birth to a worldwide icon named Harriet Tubman.

6

SLAVE CLOTHING

As stated earlier, when enslaved people were stolen from their homes in Africa, they were stripped of their clothing, as was Minty's grandmother, Modesty. They were then boarded below decks on ships for their crossing, which could take several months, following weeks in underground dungeons.

It was left to the slaveholders' discretion to clothe and feed their property according to where they worked, whether in the fields or the plantation house tending to their enslavers' children. Clothing for an enslaved child was nothing more than a gunnysack with holes cut out at the top for their head and at the sides for their arms. They were not permitted to wear underwear, even during the winter cold. If gunnysacks needed to be washed, enslaved children would remain naked until they were dry.

Clothing was made of homespun cotton and a jean cloth—a wool and cotton blend, not necessarily tailored or comfortable. Slaveholders felt their responsibility was to distribute clothing only twice a year, shoes included, and very simple clothes for children consisting of gowns or gunnysacks, depending on their age. Girls were permitted to don dresses as they grew into young women, and boys were allowed to wear short pants. Plain leather shoes were handed out along with hats for men and women. The women preferred wearing cloth headwraps according to their West African traditions.

If clothes or shoes became worn out between the twice-a-year distributions, it was up to the enslaved people to make do with what they had. That meant using twine to hold their shoes together or going barefoot in the fields if their shoes were too uncomfortable—which was very often the case.

Not much thought was given to how well the dresses or pants fit. The same went for weather conditions and seasons. Some enslavers were generous enough to give them lighter-weight clothing for the hot, humid summer months and wool clothing for the winter months. If an enslaved person was very fortunate, they received a coat, shoes, and a blanket, once in a great while, from their slaveholder.

Some enslavers supplied the enslaved people with needles, thread, and extra fabric for necessary repairs. If an enslaved woman was an attendant to the woman of the household, she would be better dressed than the others, especially the field hands. Field hands, regardless of whether they were male or female, received the cheapest clothing. The women field hands wore simple garments made of the cheapest cotton. They were not intended to last long, hence the availability of needles and thread.

We can only imagine how Modesty struggled with keeping her baby, Henrietta, or Rit, as she was nicknamed, clothed and fed while working in the fields and the Big House until her usefulness ran out.

We know there was very little to no interaction between mother and child as the children grew and were put to work in the fields, separate from their parents. There's no information on Rit's life until she reached adulthood and married Ben Ross. They began having children, and they named their fifth child Araminta (Minty).

7

A DEVIL IN THE NEIGHBORHOOD: PATTY CANNON

W hile Minty was a young child in Dorchester, growing up on the Eastern Shore of Maryland, she and her extraordinarily imaginative mind were aware of evil lurking nearby. It might explain why she spent so much time with her father, Ben, who was freed early on, leaving the Brodess plantation and going to the Thompson farm.

Minty was still years from becoming renowned for her work as a conductor on the Underground Railroad. In the years leading up to her work, we know Minty and her family endured many hardships surviving as enslaved people, as had her ancestors before her. Not as much is known about those who operated in the darkness of another type of lucrative slave trade that ran in Dorchester County. Occasionally, a benevolent plantation owner felt the impulse to grant freedom to an enslaved person. They did so for a variety of reasons: It could be that the enslaved person had reached an age where they were no longer able to work. It was time for a replacement or, in the slaveholder's mind, they had earned their freedom.

What slaveholders could not have foreseen was that the enslaved people who had been granted their freedom ran the risk of being captured—even when they carried official, signed papers clearly stating they were free men and women—only to be kidnapped and resold into slavery. Slaveholders discovered it was occurring at an alarming rate in the Dorchester area, and what was far worse was that some of these individuals were disappearing, never to be seen again. Other plantation owners were not concerned about the disappearances of the now-freed as workers were in short supply. For them, it had become a matter of supply and demand ever since the United States Congress had banned the importation of enslaved people in 1808.

The value of human life, or rather the monetary value of the life of an enslaved person, was beginning to go over $1,000, which created a new market for kidnappers who sought out formerly enslaved people in the South, forming gangs that roamed the Maryland-Delaware border. This was the same Eastern Shore area where young Minty grew up on the Brodess plantation. It was also near the Thompson farm, where she spent a great deal of time with her father, Ben, learning celestial navigation and the ways of herbal medicine. There is no way to know how aware Minty or Ben was of the gang's activity or whether Rit knew of them. But we do know about the disappearances of freed Black people that occurred before the Underground Railroad, and it is likely that all freed people were constantly vigilant against such threats.

A woman named Patty Cannon was the most notorious gang leader of her time, kidnapping freed enslaved people and selling them to slaveholders. She kidnapped the enslaved from plantations in Delaware, mainly the Eastern Shore, and resold them to plantations in Maryland—or vice versa.

Patty was married to a farmer, Jesse, who assisted in the slave-stealing trade in Dorchester County near the Brodess plantation. Victim accounts, which were written up in the abolitionist journal the *African Observer*, state that captives were chained and hidden in the basement, the attic, and secret rooms in the Cannon house. Captives were taken in covered wagons to Cannon's Ferry (now known as Woodland Ferry). At the ferry, they sometimes met a schooner traveling down the Nanticoke River to the Chesapeake Bay and on to southern slave markets.

Several free Blacks lived in Cannon's area, making them targets for her gang's kidnapping. The gang had a reputation for kidnapping from as far away as Baltimore, New Jersey, and Philadelphia. They were known to kill babies and small children. They had no compunction about robbing and murdering travelers, even though their main crimes involved stealing freed Blacks or enslaved people. They stole the enslaved despite the risk from slaveholders and their protests at losing property. The fact that the Cannon gang operated close to the Brodess plantation for years while Minty was a child no doubt had an impact, as the stories passed from one plantation to the other more than likely instilled fear in the young slave children.

One can also conceive of the palpable sense of relief that must have passed through the region when Patty Cannon was apprehended by the authorities and indicted in May of 1822. Patty was found dead in her cell on May 11, 1829.

8

MINTY'S EARLY LIFE

A raminta, or "Minty" as her parents nicknamed her, was born on the Brodess plantation, Dorchester County, Maryland, in approximately 1822. John Green had sold Modesty in a gentleman's agreement to the Brodess family. Mary Pattison Brodess initially enslaved Rit and her children, and her son, Edward Brodess, continued it. Ben was enslaved by Anthony Thompson, who became Mary's second husband and ran a large plantation nearby.

Due to heavy debt, Edward Brodess sold off several of Rit's daughters—Linah, Mariah, Sophe, and Rachael—permanently separating the family. Sophe's daughter, Ann Marie was left behind in the care of Rit and Ben. Minty never forgot the image of her sisters being taken away to another slaveholder. Her last memory of them was of all of them crying while she watched from a distance as they were carried off in a horse-drawn wagon. She never saw them again.

From the age of six onward, during the winters, Minty was expected to set, maintain, and regularly check traps for muskrats, which could be found near the waterways and whose pelts fetched high prices at the market. It did not matter that she was not effectively clothed against the harsh winter weather; her life and health were seen as insignificant—far less valuable than the muskrat pelts because there would always be another person to replace her.

Edward Brodess regularly attempted to rent out Minty to other slave-holders, always depicting her as a strong, healthy young woman, forcing her to pull horse-drawn plow equipment before potential clients to demonstrate her strength. What Brodess omitted was that Minty had suffered a severe head injury when she was approximately twelve years of age. She was picking up supplies for her slaveholder in the market with her mother, when an overseer threw a heavy weight at a young boy for no reason. Minty stepped in front of him to block the object. The weight smashed against her skull, cracking it. If Rit had not been there, Minty might have died from the bleeding on her skull. Her mother used the herbal remedies she always had on her to keep her daughter alive: allium, yarrow, and echinacea.

As it was, the injury caused significant lifelong damage, including narcolepsy, occasional seizures, and constant intense head pain. Minty might be in mid-conversation, fall asleep, awaken, and pick up right where she had left off without missing a beat. Her disability could have been a weakness—instead, Minty physically strengthened herself.

Minty was often teased by other children on the plantation for regularly falling asleep without notice. Despite this, she worked in the fields. She tended to the needs of the slaveholder's baby nightly, along with her everyday household cleaning duties. Since Minty worked in the fields and the plantation house, she may have been given two sets of clothing, one outfit for each task. Minty may have also been given leather shoes, and if they wore out, she would have either used twine to hold them together or gone barefoot in the fields. In later years, shoes were gradually improved, adding a wooden sole for durability and keeping the leather uppers intact.

The slaveholders never eased up on their demands on those enslaved on the plantation. If they felt anyone was being neglectful, they summarily whipped them. At times, Minty was beaten so severely for incorrectly cleaning that it was questionable whether she would survive. A kind plantation woman took pity on her. She carefully instructed Minty on how to clean and use a broom to prevent further beatings. Even though Minty had a severe head injury, her intelligence came through; she quickly picked up skills after being shown once and easily carried them out. Even though Minty never learned to read or write, she did not permit these factors to stand in the way of accomplishing any task.

During her youth, Minty developed a kind of faith where she conversed with God as naturally as she would speak with the person next to her. This conversational faith carried her through lonely times, whether toiling in the fields, rocking a baby to sleep, or endeavoring to please whichever master she hoped would not beat her. She dreamed of one day escaping, clueless about how she might accomplish it, but feeling in her bones that it may be possible.

During Minty's teenage years on the Thompson farm—a place she adored visiting—Minty spent quality time with her father, Ben, who worked in timber sales; his wood was transported to mariners in Baltimore for shipbuilding. Minty accompanied her father on several sales trips, meeting ship captains who introduced her to the nearby waterways. All this information was tucked away in Minty's photographic memory.

During these visits, Ben found time to teach his daughter celestial navigation and about the extensive waterways and neighboring wood-lands. While walking in the woods, Ben pointed out the medicinal roots and plants needed to heal various diseases naturally, complementing the knowledge Rit may have passed down to Minty. Rit's mother, Modesty, had learned these skills in Ghana. This raises the question of how much might have been passed on to Minty through her mother as well as her father. No one could have imagined that what Ben added to his daughter's skill set would save many lives, including his family's. In addition, Ben saw to it that Minty's physical strength increased by teaching her how to chop wood for his thriving timber business. This included clearing out trees on the farm. With any physical deficit, exercise lifts the mind, body, and spirit. Who knows whether Ben intentionally chose a strenuous activity for his barely five-foot daughter to offset the effects of her severe head injury? Whatever the case, it served her well in her future ventures.

A restlessness grew within Minty as time elapsed, even though she enjoyed being with her father for brief stints. It gave her a break from the chores of the Brodess plantation, which were often coupled with beat-ings, no matter how much effort she exerted in her tasks. Around 1849, shortly after Minty recovered from an unknown lengthy illness, Edward Brodess passed away, leaving the plantation in complete upheaval. Many of Minty's brothers and sisters were scattered throughout the Maryland area, at different plantations, or rented out. Some had ended up in chain gangs, as had other enslaved people. No one knew what would happen to the Brodesses' property. Would his widow, Eliza, keep the plantation or sell it? Fear ran rampant throughout the slave quarters. As hard and cruel as their lives were, some families had remained together, and they had an idea of what the next few minutes would bring. Now they had no clue what sunup meant for their future.

Minty and her eight brothers and sisters had been somewhat fortunate in that regard up until Edward Brodess's death. Edward had kept most of them together on his own plantation until Eliza Brodess moved her mother and siblings to his farm in Bucktown, Maryland. Minty's father, Ben, had not been sold to Edward, so he remained on the Thompson farm until he was freed sometime around 1840.

When Minty's father, Ben, had been set free and she heard that Brodess had left a will liberating her, her mother, and her siblings, Minty's hopes briefly rose. But Eliza adamantly refused to honor the will, trapping all of them.

Five years before Brodess's death, in 1844, when Minty was approxi-mately twenty-five, she had married John Tubman, a freeborn man whom she had met a few years earlier on a nearby plantation in Dorchester County, Maryland. Minty had chosen to take his last name, even though it was not a happy marriage. Edward Brodess had willingly permitted the union, as it was a marriage that was more of a convenient partnership. Even though marriages between enslaved people were honored by slaveholders, they were not regarded as binding or officially recognized, even between a freeborn and an enslaved person. The enslaved spouse could still be sold at will. But danger lurked in an unexpected place. Minty could not have known what

John had in store for her as she began to conjure up the framework of an escape plan.

Although discord had always existed between the couple, she had done her level best, in the Ashanti tradition, to keep the marriage on track. John had developed a nasty habit of publicly and privately mocking her disabilities stemming from her head injury, especially if Minty was struggling with a task, if she was unable to keep up, or if a joke went over her head.

According to family lore, as has been orally passed down through the generations, John became aware of Minty's plan to escape north with two of her brothers. She had initially intended for John to join her. He had flatly refused since he was freeborn. If he was caught with her, he would be arrested and instantly enslaved. The family further believes that John may have threatened to turn Minty in if a bounty was posted on her. He thought her escape plan was foolish. As it turns out, John was correct; a bounty of $100 had been placed on Minty's head.

Rumors circulated that a new owner was taking over the plantation, promising the enslaved would not be sold out of state and that most of the enslaved people would remain on the plantation. This seemingly good news assuaged the fears of most, but not Minty, who turned to her God conversations. Her inner voice warned her to "rise and flee!" She had no doubt they were in danger and feared that if they waited to find out if her instincts were correct, it might be too late. This was the first of many times Minty received instinctual insights and, to her advantage, she immediately trusted them. John Tubman never believed in his wife's visions or inner voice; again, he attributed them to her injury. He thought they were hallucinations. But Minty began to regard her people as Israelites and the land to the south as Egypt. The Promised Land was north, and she knew in her heart they had to head there. She could wait no longer.

9

MIND'S EYE

W hispers began to fly, within days of the plantation being sold, that Minty and her remaining sisters and brothers were to be sent to a plantation far to the south. It was the autumn of 1849, and Minty was in her mid-twenties. Her worst fears had indeed come to fruition; she was going to be separated from her parents—something she could not bear. Even though she and John were married, she would be forced away from her husband as well. Her decision was being made for her. In her heart, she knew what had to be done—it was time to put into action the lessons her father had taught her. Minty knew her father had faith in her, and she could converse with God along the way. Convincing her brothers was another concern. She questioned their determination and needed to make the argument to them that their collective lives were at stake. The enslaved were not ever permitted to speak with each other, so the conversation had to be brief and away from prying eyes. Minty managed both and got the point across to her two brothers. The decision was made to leave for the North late that very evening.

The only form of communication between enslaved people that masters ignored was singing. They could insert various words in their songs to safely pass messages that only the enslaved people could interpret. As with the Ashanti culture, music was a central theme among the enslaved. They sang hymns and created songs with spiritual themes about their labor to get them through their day. The night Minty chose to leave with her brothers, she sang:

When that ar ole chariot comes,
I'm gwine to lebe you
I'm boun' for de promised land,
Frien's, I'm gwine to lebe you.

Passing more slave cabins, Minty's well-known voice lingered while singing her message of departure:

I'm sorry, frien's to lebe you,
Farewell! Oh, farewell!
But I'll meet you in de mornin',
I'll meet you in de mornin',
When you reach de promised land;
On de oder side of Jordan,
For I'm bound for de promised land.

With the words of her song lingering in the night air, Minty and her two brothers, Ben and Henry, were gone. The trio had yet to venture far when her brothers became unnerved by the territory's newness and the unknown in the wilderness. They said goodbye to Minty and turned back to meet whatever their fate might be, leaving Minty to follow the north star, her guide on the journey ahead. As she began her walk toward freedom, she thought, "I had reasoned dis out in my mind; there was one of two things I had a right to, Liberty or death. If I could not have one, I would have de udder. For no man should take me alive. I should fight for my Liberty if my strength lasted, and when de time came for me to go, de Lord would let dem take me." Her unwavering determination and courage in the face of uncertainty is genuinely admirable.

Her father's lessons assisted her as she walked through unfamiliar wooded terrain by night. Minty recalled the invaluable time spent with her father on the Thompson farm, traversing the property in the late evening while he taught her the importance of celestial navigation. No matter where she was, Ben had reassured her she would never get lost if she followed the stars. He had also taught her how to gently feel for moss with her fingertips on tree trunks, which would aid her in determining a northerly direction on cloudy nights, as moss grows on the shaded side, away from direct sunlight, and insisted if she followed streams, they would lead to a larger body of water. He instilled in her trust in her natural, strong instincts.

Minty utilized her father's lessons as she carefully made her way along at night and did her best to hide during the day, even though the trees were beginning to lose their leaves. She may have been able to cover herself with some of the fallen leaves as the chill of fall had begun. But the kindness of strangers along the Underground Railroad, many of whom were Quakers, truly saved her. They provided her with food, dry clothes, and shelter and introduced her to a support network that would last for years.

Minty more than likely left the Brodess plantation with nothing other than the clothes she was wearing—a scratchy cotton dress that the slave-holders supplied only once or twice a year, the shoes on her feet, and, more than likely, a wrap on her head. Her shoes would have been thin leather or possibly the latest, with a wooden sole. Minty may have had stockings on her feet to ward off the crisp, cool fall weather as she headed to Phila-delphia, the land of the free.

She would have slept on the ground, curling up beneath bushes, without anything to lay her head on. Minty had never felt more alone than she now did, out in the middle of nowhere, wondering where the dividing line of freedom was. How would she know when she had crossed over it? She climbed mountains and forded rivers and streams, her feet and clothing getting soaked, and finally, after skirting the Delaware Bay, she ended her journey to freedom outside Philadelphia. Minty could not have been aware that she had walked approximately one hundred and forty miles in unfamiliar territory on sheer faith and determination. She peered at her hands to see if she was the same person, a person who had endured so much and yet remained strong.

A Mason Dixon Line crownstone marker

Unless Minty was standing next to one of the many stone markers set a mile apart along the northern and southern bounds, she would have had no confirmation she had crossed the Mason-Dixon Line. This boundary was surveyed and charted in the 1760s by Charles Mason, an astronomer, and Jeremiah Dixon, a surveyor who had delineated the legal border between Maryland and Pennsylvania before the American Revolution. Additionally, they had determined that Delaware Bay would be the eastern border. Many enslaved people had used mile-marker stones to verify they had crossed the demarcation line for their freedom.

Minty wanted to feel joy in her freedom, but knowing her parents and siblings remained enslaved left her conflicted and with a resolve; she had to discover a means to return and bring them to safety.

10

SLAVE BIBLE

M inty held onto her resolve to return and free her people, the people she had learned to refer to as Israelites from a tender age. All enslaved people on most plantations were required to attend regular Bible readings. We know most of the enslaved people were unable to read or write. Therefore, they would not know if what the slaveholders were reading was the accurate and complete Bible or if passages were intentionally omitted. There were a few enslaved people, here and there, who were taught by their slaveholders to read and write. Frederick Douglass was one of those rare few who had learned to read—his slaveholder had taught him to read and write as an adult. Later, he became one of Minty's closest friends and one of her greatest advocates.

We now know that Minty had gleaned her early references to the Israelites and Egypt from the Bible slaveholders read. Those passages remained with her, as did the stories of Moses leading his people out of Egypt to a better and safer life. It makes sense that those passages about Moses rescuing the Israelites from the grips of the Egyptians were often quoted by Minty now that we know their origins. Minty had heard the words read since her early childhood

During the time of Minty and her forebears, most slaveholders were Christian and held a belief in the Bible. The original Slave Bible was brought from the British West Indies in 1807 and found its way onto the southern colonial American plantations before Minty's birth. This version of the Bible was written three years following the Haitian Revolution. The words from this book varied from the African heritage many enslaved people had been forced to leave behind. Some enslaved may have begun to listen to what was being read by their masters out of desperation, even if it conflicted with their original African beliefs. The slaveholders taught them that the Bible insisted it was God's will that there be slaves. It was their God-given right to own, buy, and sell enslaved people, and the slaveholders insisted the Bible said as much. They further claimed that the Bible said God ordered enslaved people to be obedient to their masters. Masters read those passages repeatedly to the enslaved people. Who could argue with either the master or the book they read from?

With about half of the New Testament deleted, the slaveholders held the belief it had the power to keep the potential of a slave rebellion down. They also felt that if the enslaved accepted their lot in life, they would be more adjusted to their station and become better enslaved people. Slaveholders relied on this redacted and edited Bible to be a warped word of God to teach their slaves obedience. The Slave Bible did include the enslavement of Joseph in Egypt. It referred to his faith in God and, in turn, understanding his position in life.

It is unknown who initially decided to alter the Bible before it arrived from the British West Indies and made it to the Colonies. There are several schools of thought, one of which points to the British and the other to the missionaries. In either case, the underlying message of the Slave Bible, of which there is one on display at the Museum of the Bible in Washington, DC, is that of strict obedience of the enslaved to their masters.

Anything remotely related to equality among men was removed from the Slave Bible, as was the Book of Revelations. However, all passages referring to enslaved people obeying their masters remained and were read and reread.

But whatever Bible was read to Minty had passages in it that dealt with the Israelites being led to freedom. These Liberation passages of the Slave Bible drove Minty in her quest, especially when coupled with those passages that spoke to pro-abolitionism, like healing the sick and brokenhearted, helping the poor, and preaching deliverance to captives. Decades later, these words would also become part of the platform for the suffragettes, in which Minty, as a free woman, would come to play a significant role.

Frederick Douglass had his own thoughts on how religion was manipulated to justify enslavement, which appeared in chapter XI of his 1892 book, *Life and Times of Frederick Douglass* (1892):

> I have met many good religious colored people in the South who were under the delusion that God required them to submit to slavery and to wear their chains with meekness and humility. I could entertain no such nonsense as this, and I entirely lost my patience when I found a colored man weak enough to believe such stuff. Nevertheless, eager as I was to partake of the tree of knowledge, its fruits were bitter and sweet. "Slaveholders," thought I, "are only a band of successful robbers who, leaving their own homes, went into Africa to steal and reduce my people to slavery; I loathed them as the meanest and the most wicked of men."

Frederick Douglass

In later years, Douglass added an appendix to his book; a portion of it follows:

> Slaveholding Religion and the Christianity of Christ
>
> I find, since reading over the preceding Narrative, that I have, in several instances, spoken in such a tone and manner, respecting religion, as may lead those unacquainted with religious views to suppose me an opponent of all religion. To remove the liability of such misapprehension, I deem it proper to append the following brief explanation. What I have said respecting and against religion, I mean to surely apply to the slaveholding religion of this land, and with no possible reference to Christianity proper; for, between the possible difference—so wide, that to receive the one as good, pure, and holy, is of necessity to reject the other as bad, corrupt, and wicked. To be the friend of and impartial Christianity of Christ: I, therefore, hate the corrupt, slaveholding, women-whipping, cradle-plundering, partial and hypocritical Christianity of this land.

Minty, however, was not placated by redacted or piecemeal Bible passages. She had heard the passages detailing Moses leading the Israelites to freedom and, coupled with her own spiritual conversations with God, they strengthened her conviction that she had a different path to follow.

11

FUGITIVE SLAVE ACT

Minty arrived in Philadelphia in the fall of 1849 without a penny to her name. Pennsylvania was a free state, giving her the unique experience of walking the streets without fear of being captured by slave catchers or those who had joined their newly organized local slave patrols and wore badges to distinguish themselves from slave catchers. To honor her newfound freedom and to honor her mother, Minty decided to change her name from Araminta to her mother's name, Harriet.

To pursue her dream of returning to Maryland, freeing her family, and bringing her husband north, Harriet needed to find employment. Harriet had an extensive skill set that qualified her for all sorts of employment besides domestic chores, which she had acquired through her work on the plantation. She had farmed, tended to children, trapped muskrats, chopped wood, and excelled at anything she set her mind to accomplishing. Harriet no longer had to answer to a master and wondered if she could be paid for her abilities. As good luck would have it, Harriet discovered that not only could she make and save money as a domestic worker, but some good people were willing to assist her with finding housing and purchasing adequate clothes. All this new information coincided with her meeting a Black man named William Still.

When Harriet met William Still, she could not have known he would be an introduction to a vital and extensive network of friends. William Still was born a free man in New Jersey, moved to Philadelphia in 1844, and worked for the Pennsylvania Society for the Abolition of Slavery. One of his jobs was locating housing for escaped enslaved people. His Underground Railroad Station stop was rather popular with escaped enslaved people who were going to Canada. In the years he worked his route, it is estimated he assisted approximately eight hundred people to freedom. He destroyed most of his meticulous notes, fearing the possibility of escaped enslaved people being recaptured. In later years, his children encouraged him to write one of the more accurate depictions of the era: *The Underground Railroad*, published in 1872. His reassurance of and assistance to Harriet, coupled with the years he spent housing and aiding her as she traveled back and forth, were invaluable. Conductors of the Underground Railroad like William Still were the unsung heroes of the era, displaying immense bravery and selflessness in their efforts to help others.

William Still referred to Harriet as the "Moses" of her people in his writings and in speaking to others, since she referred to Maryland as "Egypt." The nickname Moses was given to Harriet around 1858 by a White abolitionist, William Lloyd Garrison, who owned and published *The Liberator*, an abolitionist newspaper that ran both before and during the Civil War. Garrison's nickname for Harriet has held to this very day. We don't know if Garrison knew Harriet had a younger brother who bore the name Moses.

Harriet worked as many hours as humanly possible to save as much money as she could. She knew the costs would mount quickly as she traveled back to Bucktown, Maryland, to rescue her family members. Her dependence on the Underground Railroad would go only so far on the return trip, and what would they do if they had to go beyond Philadelphia? Harriet had heard talk of Congress passing a Fugitive Slave Act, meaning either slave catchers or the slave patrols could cross into northern territory and capture runaway slaves. If the act became the law of the land, it would dramatically alter the landscape, making saving lives much more complex,

Underground Railroad or not. Saving even more money became her central focus. Harriet had to depart Philadelphia in a rush and immediately head back to her homeland, Maryland, before the Fugitive Slave Act could be passed.

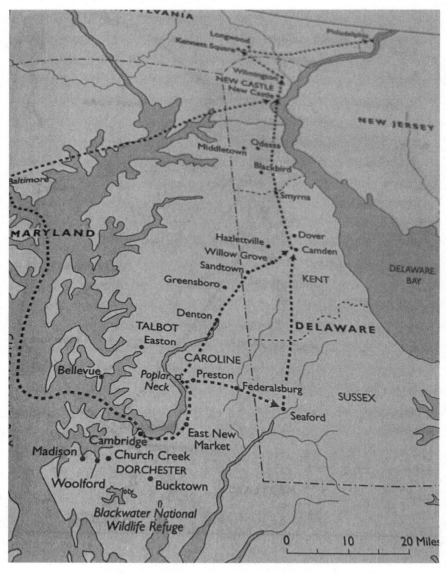

Harriet Tubman's Southern Underground Railroad routes to Philadelphia

Many Philadelphians were ready to help Harriet and played a significant part in the Railroad, many of whom were Quakers. These Quakers, driven by their commitment to social justice, were prepared at a moment's notice to assist whenever asked, even if it was in the middle of the night.

One of Harriet's close Quaker allies was Lucretia Mott, the famed suffragist, who made herself available to Harriet throughout her life. Numerous other Quakers aided Harriet and thousands of enslaved people on their way to freedom. Not all their names are known since there were approximately eighty in Chester County, Pennsylvania, alone. By 1850, more than three thousand people were working with the Underground Railroad, reaching from the South through Iowa, Michigan, Indiana, Ohio, New York, Massachusetts, and up to Canada. The Quakers' dedication to the cause of freedom and justice was a beacon of hope in a dark time, inspiring many others to join the fight.

Lucretia Mott and Levi Coffin were among some of the more well-known people who worked with Harriet. A man known as Thomas Garrett was a Station master in Wilmington, Delaware, and worked on the Railroad for roughly forty years. Despite being fined more than $5,400 for his involvement in helping 2,700 people escape slavery, he pushed forth. Coffin was based in Cincinnati, Ohio, and was known as the president of the Underground Railroad.

Not all Quakers agreed with harboring enslaved people along the Railroad; they were in favor of abolition through legal means. This meant freeing all enslaved people, as opposed to focusing their efforts on the relatively few who attempted escape. Even so, records indicate that by the middle of the nineteenth century, over 50,000 enslaved people had escaped from the South, making use of the Underground Railroad.

Plantation owners exerted their power of persuasion over Congress. In response, Congress passed the Fugitive Slave Act in 1850, a law that required all escaped slaves, upon capture, to be returned to their masters and imposed penalties on anyone who aided in their escape. This brought about a new industry of slave catchers, who became known as bounty hunters and were permitted to use whatever means necessary to trap runaways and cash in on a lucrative business. It did not have the intended result of ending the Underground Railroad; instead, it became an incentive for the conductors to be more secretive and imaginative. It reinforced Harriet's resolve to journey back to her homeland, Maryland, and rescue her family members quickly. Harriet had her visions, her God conversations, the physical strength her father had fostered, and the knowledge he had imparted to her to rely upon. She had her Ashanti heritage to guide her, coupled with the network of the Underground Railroad at her disposal; Harriet had all the necessary tools to make the treacherous journey back South.

12

SONGS OF CODE

S inging was not just a means of communication that Harriet had grown up with but a powerful tool that uplifted her spirit. She was taught that it was a significant part of her Ashanti heritage with a dual purpose: a form of spiritual expression and a way to exchange coded messages. Singing also passed the time while working in the fields, planting, or setting muskrat traps by herself. She often sang to the master's babies to help them fall asleep at night, a testament to the power of music to inspire and bring hope even in the darkest times.

Singing was not just a pastime for enslaved people. It became a strategic tool in their quest for freedom. They composed songs about their work, not only to pass the time but also to motivate themselves. Over time, these songs evolved into covert communication, with specific lyrics and melodies carrying hidden messages. They contained specific directions, guiding enslaved people to designated meeting points where they could gather and plan their escape to the North.

Harriet, a beacon of bravery, became known for her specific songs, including "Swing Low Sweet Chariot." It told the enslaved people who heard her singing to be ready to escape, as the Underground Railroad was preparing to assist them.

It was one of Harriet's favorite songs. This song carried the weight of her hopes and dreams for freedom, a song that she sang with a mixture of fear and determination, a song that echoed through the fields and the hearts of the enslaved people:

Swing low, sweet chariot,
Coming to carry me home,
Swing low, sweet chariot,
Coming for to carry me home.
I looked over Jordan and what did I see
Coming for to carry me home,
A band of angels coming after me,
Coming for to carry me home.
If you get there before I do,
Coming for to carry me home,
Tell all my friends that I'm coming too,
Coming for to carry me home.

Harriet was astutely aware of specific warning signals to the enslaved, and how to use them to keep her people safe, that enslavers would not comprehend:

(Chorus)
Oh go down, Moses,
Way down into Egypt's land,
Tell old Pharaoh,
Let my people go.
Oh Pharaoh said he would go cross,
Let my people go,
And don't get lost in the wilderness,
Let my people go.
(Chorus)
You may hinder me here, but you can't up there,

Let my people go,
He sits in the Heaven and answers prayers,
Let my people go!

Harriet's singing of "Wade in the Water" was intended to instruct the enslaved people she had in her charge to head into a nearby stream if and when the slave catchers with bloodhounds were close by. She had learned long ago the water would disguise their scent:

Wade in the Water. God's gonna trouble the water.
Who are those children all dressed in Red?
God's gonna trouble the water.
Must be the ones that Moses led.
God's gonna trouble the water.
(Chorus)
Who are those children all dressed in White?
God's gonna trouble the water
Must be the ones of the Israelites.
God's gonna trouble the water.
(Chorus)
Who are those children all dressed in Blue?
God's gonna trouble the water.
Must be the ones who made it through.
God's gonna trouble the water.

"Follow the Drinking Gourd" was a song that would have been heard in the spring. The words go with the lessons in celestial navigation Ben had wisely taught his daughter all those years ago, when she was a teenager, back when she went by the name Minty. The drinking gourd is code for the Big Dipper, which points to the north. The song mentions the quail, who begin calling each other in April. It also refers to dead trees. Once again, we are reminded of Ben's navigational lessons: he had taught her to feel for the moss on the trees, even if they were dead. She knew that was the north side of the tree, even if it was dark or too cloudy to observe the Big Dipper:

I when the Sun comes back
And the first quail calls
Follow the Drinking Gourd.
For the old man is a-waiting for to carry you to freedom
If you follow the Drinking Gourd.
The riverbank makes a very good road.
The dead trees will show you the way.
Left foot, peg foot, traveling on,
Follow the Drinking Gourd.
The river ends between two hills
Follow the Drinking Gourd.
There's another river on the other side
Follow the Drinking Gourd.
When the great big river meets the little river
Follow the Drinking Gourd.
For the old man is a-waiting for to carry you to freedom
If you follow the Drinking Gourd.

Harriet's return journey was far different than her escape. She had gone north without a cent to her name, no additional clothing, and, crucially, no support network. The Underground Railroad ran the entire route from Philadelphia to Maryland, and Harriet's photographic memory now knew every single step of the way. William Still and other conductors informed her of each Station's location. Her infirmity since childhood would not stop her from the mission at hand; she would bring her family and many others who sought freedom back along the Railroad Trail.

Quaker Station conductors were known to light lamps in their doorways in the evening to alert escaped enslaved people to whether it was safe to seek refuge with them. If the lamp was unlit, it was a silent code informing them that bounty hunters were nearby and that they should remain hidden for the time being. Harriet understood that when she saw that an expected lamp was dark, it meant she had to forgo a meal and lodging. If there was inclement weather, she had to sleep underneath bushes and cover herself with whatever she carried. If bounty hunters were wandering about, their footfalls frequently awakened her. Sometimes, she had difficulty sleeping, fearing she would be discovered, captured, returned to the plantation, and harshly punished. Slaveholders were not above making an example of runaway slaves. Harriet was determined not to be among that number; she had every intention of rescuing her entire family.

Harriet moved swiftly with heightened awareness and excitement. It had been a year since she had seen her husband, parents, or siblings. She wondered how they were as she walked at night and hid during the day. This first trip was to bring her husband, John Tubman, with her to Philadelphia. They had been unable to have children, adding to the unhappiness of the marriage, but a move could change things. Harriet had no clue how disillusioned she was about to become.

Harriet found John but, to her utter shock and dismay, discovered that he had married another woman, Caroline. He had told Harriet before she had left Maryland that he did not want to accompany her. Yet she had not dreamed that his refusal included his taking another wife. John had waited barely a year before marrying Caroline. Harriet could not have known that John would be shot and killed by a White man in a roadside argument sixteen years later, leaving behind four children. His killer would be found not guilty by an all-White jury.

Harriet had never experienced such a deep betrayal. She had to set it aside, find her inner strength and move forward. She could not allow her mission to go to waste. Harriet quietly moved around the plantation, from slave quarters to slave quarters, singing familiar hymns to gather enslaved people seeking freedom. Her zeal paid off; she safely guided a small group of enslaved people along the Railroad to their freedom. They traveled north the way she had—walking by night and finding shelter if they could during the day. Bounty hunters with bloodhounds were everywhere, scurrying through the brush, over rugged mountain passes, and through rivers as Harriet and her group were relentlessly chased. Harriet did her best to keep to the streams and rivers whenever possible, to avoid leaving a scent behind for the dogs to follow; it was a trick she had learned from some caring Quakers.

Although Harriet was guiding a large group, the bounty hunters had difficulty keeping up with them. Some in the hunter's group fell far behind, while others tripped over fallen trees, injured themselves, or simply gave up from fatigue. Harriet, at one time, may have had a bounty of as much as $400 on her head; however, nothing could make one move faster than being responsible for others' lives, including babies'. Even though she had barely begun her conductor days, Harriet was not about to run a "train" off a track. She knew she would make many more trips back to Egypt, once this group settled, with the backing of William Still and many others along the Railroad.

She took her calling as the Moses of her people to heart, believing it was her duty to free as many enslaved as possible so long as she was alive. Harriet continued to have her visions, which indicated that saving lives was indeed her life's work. She had to take the time to work between missions to save the necessary funds for each journey. Dependence on the Quakers' and others' generosity would take her only so far. Occasionally, unexpected expenses arose, and Harriet had to pay for them—horses and buggies to carry and hide her charges, feed for the horses, and numerous riverboat crossings. Occasionally, she was stopped by riverboat captains who were friendly to the cause and allowed her and her group passage on their ferries. Not everyone in the South was pro-slavery.

On one journey, Harriet nearly bumped into an old master near a train station. Fearing he might recognize her, even though she was wearing a bonnet, she bent down to pick up a couple of loose chickens that had gotten away from a nearby vendor and released them near her old master. While his arms flapped at the chickens, Harriet hurriedly walked in the opposite direction. In another instance, she was on a train. Once again fearful of being recognized, she picked up a newspaper and pretended to read it. Unable to read or write, Harriet unintentionally held the paper upside down. None of the passengers appeared to notice. Harriet later related these stories to audiences, post-slavery and post–Civil War, when she was in high demand as a speaker to abolitionists and suffragettes.

Harriet made numerous trips to "Egypt," continuing to rescue the enslaved and bring them to freedom, before she could make it to her own family, whom she hoped were still in Dorchester. It haunted her that she could free so many others but not her flesh and blood. Harriet often speculated who remained alive, which of her brothers and sisters had been sold to other plantations, and whether or not she would ever be reunited with them. She had vague memories of her grandmother, Modesty, moments before her passing and did not want that to occur with her parents and her siblings. She held to her Ashanti teachings, her God conversations, and what her father, Ben, had imparted; she had to be strong for them.

As they headed north, one central Station stopping point for Harriet and those in her care was Thomas Garrett's home. He took enormous risks to shelter escaped enslaved people on their way to freedom and was always happy to lend a helping hand to Harriet. He not only provided food and clothing but if his Station was under the watch of bounty hunters, he escorted them to a more secure location.

Thomas Garrett, a Quaker, was the son of Quakers. He was raised on a farm in Upper Darby, Delaware County, Pennsylvania. The Garrett family farm had become known as "Thornfield." He and his younger brother Edward developed a reputation for hiding and aiding fugitive slaves. They followed a family tradition of participating in the anti-slavery movement dating back to the middle 1770s, a tradition in which Thomas and Edward took immense pride.

Thomas Garrett had the local distinction of regularly hiding runaway enslaved individuals. When slave catchers learned that runaways had headed to Garrett's, they gave up, knowing all the enslaved people would be well concealed.

Thomas Garrett

Thomas was all in when assisting the runaway enslaved. He never minded not being praised for his work, and he tolerated threats of imprisonment and hefty fines. Once, a reward for his arrest was set at $10,000 by the state of Maryland. A Maryland Supreme Court justice later fined him after he announced to the court that he had indeed aided the fugitive enslaved. He further stated he had no intention of changing his ways.

Garrett took personal pride in being fined. Some say it challenged him to carry on running a Railroad stop. Whatever the fine was, it was worth it to help all those people to freedom.

Due to these hefty fines, Thomas became bankrupt despite being a wealthy man with a successful business. Thomas Garrett had something neither judges nor slave catchers could take from him, and that was dear friends who helped him get back on his feet, reestablish his business, and carry on with the operation of his Underground Railroad Station.

Garrett wrote letters detailing the extreme conditions some of the run-aways arrived in, including Harriet Tubman. He recounted that she never kept the money she earned for herself but spent it on others, especially for return trips to "Egypt." He wrote, "Harriet and one of the men had worn their shoes off their feet, and I gave them two dollars to help fit them out and directed a carriage to be hired at my expense."

Every trip south to Egypt was risky for Harriet. Still, the return trip to Philadelphia was even more hazardous due to the passage of the Fugitive Slave Act of 1850, which included not just Pennsylvania, but New York as well. The protection of William Still did not matter anymore, as Harriet was a runaway and subject to capture. With a large bounty on her, slave catchers were roaming the streets, keeping a close watch for her. It was up to her to find another route to freedom for her people, and she soon understood that the only remaining pathway led to Canada. She would need to purchase horses and wagons and was able to do so with her savings because of having performed domestic work and saved wisely, coupled with the generosity of Thomas Garrett and others.

In her next mission north, these horses and wagons would prove to be invaluable. Some enslaved people could walk the distance, whereas others would take turns riding and walking the long and dangerous path to Canada.

13

SHOES ARE MADE FOR WALKING

A young enslaved man named Joe worked extremely hard for his master. He possessed extraordinary strength, and he was of above-average height. It did not matter how much effort he put forth in his tasks; his master beat him relentlessly and for no reason. His master demanded Joe strip down and tolerate daily beatings; he claimed it was part of showing Joe that he was owned and had no choice other than to take the beating. Joe did as he was told and did not move an inch. Joe promised himself this torture would not be unending and that he would escape before too long. Under cover of darkness one night, he found a boat and drove downriver, on the Blackwater River, to Harriet's father's farm. Her father was known around the region as Old Ben. Joe asked Old Ben if he knew when Moses would return to the area; he wanted to go with her to freedom. By this point, Ben was a freedman; his former slaveholder's written will had clearly stated that Ben would gain his freedom upon the slaveholder's death.

Ben never saw his daughter or heard her come by the farm to collect Joe or any other enslaved people willing to leave with her. He realized she had learned her lessons well enough to enter and exit with such nimbleness under the cloak of darkness. Joe's owner came by the farm, shouting at the top of his lungs, hunting for Joe, who was nowhere to be found. Several others from nearby plantations had also gone missing, including two of Joe's brothers and one sister. Before anyone realized what had transpired, the group was long gone. They hid in all sorts of obscure places during the day while they were being closely pursued, covering themselves with leaves. Or they would backtrack in and out of streams, getting their feet wet, causing the hounds to lose their scent. Sometimes, the slave catchers came within mere feet of them. The group was rather large, so they had to separate. Several traveled by boat, some on foot, and others by wagon, until they met at a Station on the Railroad at a bridge near the Delaware River. Police officers heavily guarded the Wilmington Bridge. Postings of rewards for Joe had already been put up, initially for $1,000, and then they were increased to $2,000. There were rewards for Harriet, as well. It did not deter her; she knew she could depend on Thomas Garrett, whose Station was nearby; he had never let her down before.

Harriet led her terrified party to Thomas Garrett's home. As she had anticipated, Thomas fed and clothed every single one. Being the owner of a large shoe company, he ensured no one ever left his home without a brand-new pair of shoes, even extremely tall Joe. Thomas knew the valiant group needed warm clothing and sturdy shoes to assist them on their lengthy journey to St. Catherines across the Canadian border.

Thomas was as creative as he was generous and determined to get Harriet and her fellow travelers across the bridge, even though it was swarming with police. He sought the support of local bricklayers, who filled their wagons with bricks. They merrily drove off toward the well-fortified bridge, singing loudly and waving to the police, who permitted them to pass. Shortly after darkness fell, the bricklayers recrossed the Wilmington Bridge with an empty wagon, singing as they went.

A while later, once the darkness had become pitch black, the fugitives were lying on the bottom of the wagon as close to each other as possible. They did not move or make a sound while the men made another crossing,

singing just as before. The police had seen them twice now, and, not sus-
pecting that there was anything in their wagons other than more bricks,
they permitted them to cross without realizing they had allowed all the
enslaved people to escape. It would have ended in disaster if it had not been
for Thomas Garrett.

Although Garrett's plan had carried them without harm across the
bridge, many miles remained between them and the Canadian border,
the only place out of reach of the long arm of the Fugitive Slave Act. Harriet's reputation for never losing passengers on the Railroad had spread, and
she was not about to begin now. She was fully aware of the large bounty
on her and Joe and knew slave catchers would pursue them endlessly. As
Garrett, her friend and ally, had seen to it, they not only had clothing
and shoes but also an ample amount of money to tide them over. As they
traveled farther north, Garrett knew that the November air would turn
colder, so he had included plenty of warm coats, socks, bonnets, and hats
for everyone. He added an enormous stack of blankets, too. There were
other like-minded anti-slavery people they could depend on on the way
to freedom, who would restock the required provisions. She knew she was
not alone in her rescue efforts and always gratefully recognized the help
she received along the way.

If too much time elapsed between Harriet Tubman's trips with groups
she had rescued, Garrett had been known to pen a letter to their mutual
friend in Philadelphia, William Still, to check on her welfare. With all the
slave catchers about, Garrett wanted to be sure nothing had befallen his
dear, brave friend with all the miles he knew she had to travel.

Harriet continued to guide the weary escapees under the veil of darkness until they reached the protection of the anti-slavery office in New
York as the leaves were beginning to change colors. The weary group had
traveled roughly one hundred and fifteen miles, give or take, and they still
had well over four hundred miles remaining before reaching the safety of
St. Catherines.

When they reached New York City, a man named Oliver Johnson welcomed the travelers with open arms and, like Garrett, fed them. He was

pleased to meet Joe, whose bounty was worth $2,000. Joe was perplexed about how Oliver knew who he was until he saw his likeness on a wanted poster. He was simultaneously taken aback and frightened and inquired whether traveling all that distance was for nothing. He feared recapture and being whipped to death.

Oliver spread out the map of New York on a table for Joe and pointed to where he currently was. He informed Joe that Niagara Falls, the line of complete freedom, was three hundred miles from their current location. Oliver pulled out another map to indicate to Joe how great a distance they had remaining to travel. It had the opposite of the intended effect on Joe; he became entirely enveloped by fear. Harriet's regular cheery singing could not shake him out of it as they readied to leave Oliver's office. Joe fell into total silence. Although they had all experienced cruelty at the hands of their masters, no one could fathom what he had gone through for his master to place such an astronomical reward on his head. Oliver attempted to reassure Joe of Harriet's extraordinary ability to get all of them to freedom and that he could trust her. Joe's eyes remained full of terror.

Oliver sent them on their way, imagining he would see his dear friend Harriet again on her next trip, saving yet another weary band dreaming of living and breathing free air. He tried to envision Joe as he approached Niagara Falls and set foot on the other side, permitting the sounds of freedom to wash over him.

The Suspension Bridge eventually came into view, coupled with the sight of the promised land on the other side. It was so close they could nearly feel its warmth begin to wrap around them. They knew they were not safe from the slave catchers until their feet were on Canadian soil. The bridge may as well have been a thousand miles long, with the sound of Niagara Falls thundering above and a raging river beneath them.

The near-deafening roar brought joy to Harriet and helped drown most of the jitters her Railroad passengers felt. Joe's anxiety slowly diminished as they crossed the middle of the bridge into Canada. The realization dawned on them as their feet touched Canadian soil for the first time that they were truly free. The roaring waters of the falls persisted in the fabulous fresh, free air they inhaled deeply. The travelers burst into a joyous song, and Joe joined the chorus this time. They no longer had to dread the bounty hunters and the bloodhounds during either the night or day. They did not have to depend on the kindness of strangers to house them, the Quakers on the Underground Railroad to hide them during the day—no more hiding in the bushes in inclement weather while being hunted by armed slave catchers. Harriet's first foray into St. Catherines, with Joe and the others, became one of the most inspiring and legendary parts of her speeches to abolitionist and suffragette audiences. The courageous group, led by Harriet, had logged nearly two hundred hours of travel time—from beginning to end—a portion of it walking and some by horse-drawn wagon. It was in St. Catherines where Harriet would meet John Brown some years later. Brown was so awestruck at meeting her that he dubbed her General Tubman and referred to her as one of the best and bravest people on the planet.

These now-free people possessed skills from years of housekeeping and farming on plantations for their past masters, and that knowledge would give them a better opportunity to seek decent employment in St. Catherines, not far from where they now stood. As Harriet had honestly earned her wages in Philadelphia, they too would be paid for their labor instead of being forced to work and beaten for no reason. This had been inconceivable until Moses had rescued them.

14

THE BASE OF OPERATIONS

With her savings and the help of her supporters, Harriet was able to rent a house in St. Catherines, Ontario; it was to become her first home and base of operations. It made it possible for her to travel back and forth between the land of deliverance and Egypt to save more enslaved people and bring them to liberation. The people she rescued remained with her, paying rent and board if they were able while finding jobs in Ontario as domestics or laborers. Some stayed on as boarders, while others found their own housing, after they had been able to save sufficient funds, in what became the first African village in Canada.

One of her many stops on the Underground Railroad included the home of Senator William Seward and his wife, Francis, in Auburn, New York. They were staunch abolitionists, and they and Harriet became lifelong friends. Like others along Harriet's path, they were able to lend a hand with whatever was needed and whenever they could. This included all the necessities for those Harriet had rescued to carry through with their journey, with additional warm clothing for northern winters and plenty of food and money to give them a good start in their new life of independence. Her base of operations in the land of the now manumitted enabled Harriet to return to Maryland frequently to rescue far more of her people than she could have imagined. Having people such as the Sewards, Thomas Garrett, William Still, and Lucretia Mott made the traveling from point to point a reality, even though the danger would persist.

With each foray, Harriet learned something new regarding the terrain and the waterways that served her well on future voyages and would help with later endeavors. As her survival instincts increased, she heard bounty hunters almost before their approach. She safely hid each group as they made their way through the underbrush. Most of Harriet's missions were during the long, dark winter months—utilizing the darkness for added concealment. Another trick Harriet had learned along the way was to leave on Saturday evenings, since newspapers would not print any notices regarding the runaway enslaved until Monday morning, giving her more than a day's head start.

Traveling on holidays also gave her additional lead time. She had a Christmas mission planned, but before she departed, Harriet trusted a close friend with a request, as her illiteracy kept her from writing her few remaining enslaved brothers. She had managed to save some of her family members but was determined to bring the rest to her home in St. Catherines. Harriet thought they all belonged together, including her parents, and she would not rest until this task was accomplished. What more appropriate season for this than Christmas? The letter was sent to a friend, Jacob, and signed by William Henry Jackson. It was written in a code Harriet knew would reach her brother John. Jacob could read and write, and she trusted him to decipher her meaning. The letter instructed them to be ready for the good ship *Zion*, which was scheduled for arrival shortly. When it did show up, the brothers were to step aboard immediately. Jacob was confused as he did not have brothers. After rereading the letter, he understood it was meant for John, Harriet's brother, and the ship *Zion* would be captained by Moses, or Harriet herself. He made sure to let John know Harriet was on her way.

Harriet, per usual, appeared mysteriously, unbeknownst to anyone. Word was carefully passed to her brothers to meet at their father's cabin, Old Ben's, on Christmas night. Harriet was confident her mother, Rit, would be safe until she could be rescued later, as she was no longer of much use to the slaveholder due to her advanced age. Harriet had promised herself she would return later for her parents and get them safely to St. Catherines. This trip was explicitly intended to keep her brothers—young and strong—out of the clutches of the chain gangs in the Deep South. The possibility of never seeing them again rose exponentially if her brothers were traded or shipped. As much as Harriet desired to bring her parents north with her on this trip, she knew it would have to be postponed once more. Even though it had been six years since she had laid eyes on them, she would have to push it off longer.

Harriet patiently waited with the assembled group, minus her brother John. His wife was close to giving birth to another child, and he was filled with guilt about leaving her. He knew his options would be dire if he did not go with Moses immediately, but his wife was not aware of his predicament. He stood outside, listening to his wife cry, summoning the courage to walk several miles to his father's cabin, leaving his family behind. In his heart, he knew he would have to do this. Going north allowed him to see his family again; being sold into a chain gang did not, he told himself before meeting with Harriet and the others. And if he were free, perhaps he could help Harriet come back and fetch his wife and new child before too long.

Harriet knew her mother looked forward to Christmas and having her entire family surrounding her. It was a special day, and she spent hours cooking in anticipation of the boys' appearance. No doubt the pig had been killed and various family favorite dishes had already been carefully prepared. The boys had not yet shown up, and Harriet imagined that her mother wondered what danger had befallen them as she patiently sat in her chair and slowly rocked while waiting for them. Harriet joined two of her brothers in the fodder house, where grain and other feed for the farm animals were stored, and they anxiously awaited John's arrival. Harriet and her mother were worrying, independent of each other, wondering if the brothers had met an ugly fate.

Two other fugitives with the party went to the house to attract Ben's attention without Rit noticing. Ben briefly came out, and once he understood what was occurring, he returned inside and packaged some food on the sly. With only a few whispered words to his boys, he left the wrapped food inside the door of the fodder house. Anything more would have endangered them all. They ate in silence and sadness as John joined them. They desperately wanted to join their aging mother, but for now, it was not possible. The closest thing the siblings could do before leaving that night was go to the cabin and bid their mother a silent farewell. As they drew near, they watched her through the window, gently rocking herself beside the fire. They knew she feared the worst scenario for them. They silently cried and wished they could reassure her they were safe, that their sister Harriet was taking them out of danger. As they turned to begin their journey north, Harriet promised each of them she would return and bring their parents to safety in St. Catherines. Holding that promise in their hearts, they set off on the long walk to the next Station of the Underground Railroad. Harriet's brothers and the other fugitives trusted her knowledge of the terrain; they were keenly aware of her many successful missions in saving other escaped enslaved people, even with a cold, harsh winter coming on. They had heard stories of the generous White Quakers who had gifted those travelers before them with warm clothing, plenty of food, and more money than they had seen in a lifetime to tide them over until they found work in Canada, the land of the free. Moses consistently lifted her people into a new land of plenty.

15

PARENTS IN THE PROMISED LAND

H arriet instinctively knew the time had come. She could not set it aside any longer; she had to go down to Egypt once more to rescue her mother and father. The amount of the bounty on her head was immaterial. They were her parents. Too many years had passed since she had laid eyes on her mother, other than through a window that cold Christmas night. Harriet held her father's arm, while he was blindfolded, as they walked to the barn so he could truthfully respond, if questioned by slave catchers, that he had not seen her.

One more lengthy, dangerous journey was more than worth it. And Harriet would see her friends on the Underground Railroad—William Still, Thomas Garrett, and others—again.

Using her ingenuity, Harriet could bargain with a farmer to hire a wagon to carry her parents and their meager belongings on the extensive journey to St. Catherines. By this point, her aged mother could not walk without the assistance of a cane. The wagon allowed them to store food and clothing that anyone might donate as they traveled through Maryland and Delaware, stopping and resting at familiar Railroad destinations. Even with the wagon, the over-six-hundred-mile trip would be severely dangerous for her mother. They rested as often as necessary to rejuvenate her. Still, the poor woman was exhausted by the time they reached the Niagara Falls Suspension Bridge.

When they finally arrived in St. Catherines, the warmth of freedom offset the bitterly cold winter. They did their best to warm their old bones, mainly through the joy of reuniting with their children under one roof after so many years of separation. Old Ben and Rit could sit back at long last and relax with their children without being concerned about providing for the rest of the family.

16

AUBURN, NEW YORK, AND THE SEWARDS

Harriet made frequent trips between St. Catherines and Maryland between approximately 1850 and 1860, repeatedly outsmarting slave catchers despite risking her own life. Her deep friendship with and support from William and Frances Seward was easily sustained as the rescues and passages through Auburn continued. After great success in his private law practice, William Seward served in the US Senate following his return to politics. It was not a secret Senator Seward was anti-slavery, having clearly stated so during a lengthy Senate floor speech about the immorality of slavery. It was a natural step for him and his wife to support Harriet's missions in whatever feasible manner. Therefore, it was also a natural progression for them to assist Harriet in purchasing her own home close to them in Auburn, New York. Not traveling the extra distance to St. Catherines would greatly simplify her going back and forth to Maryland. The additional travel miles had begun to be burdensome; shortening the trip would make an enormous difference. William and Frances wanted to loan her the money. They trusted Harriet completely to repay them once she had obtained the funds.

Frances Seward

Harriet knew she was fortunate to have the backing of this influential, powerful couple—a friendship that would be a two-way street for years to come. She and Frances became dear friends, managing to separate her rescue missions from William's political life, as not everyone agreed with hiding escaped enslaved people. Many people of Auburn were unaware of the secret hideaway in the Sewards' basement, where several fugitives Harriet had brought north were safely housed until other accommodations and employment could be worked out. Despite the lingering effects of her childhood head injury, Harriet remained tireless and intent on bringing her parents to Auburn as the Canadian winters were becoming unbearable for them. She also wanted to rescue as many others as possible, especially when Senator Seward began to speak openly on the Senate floor of the potential for civil war.

The Sewards were happy to loan Harriet $1,200 to purchase a home in Auburn, New York, for her and her parents to reside in. William Seward gave Harriet ample time to repay the loan; being financially comfortable due to his highly successful law practice allowed him to wait for repayment as long as necessary. If her brothers and sisters wanted to move to Auburn, they were welcome. Changing her base of operations meant a great deal to Harriet, especially having a home of her own. Harriet quickly worked to pay the money back to the stalwart Sewards.

Harriet had plans to make a trip to Boston, but before leaving, she went to St. Catherines again to pack up her parents and their belongings a final time. She assured them they were going to their very own home, one that she, Harriet Tubman, owned—an escaped slave woman who now had a piece of property as opposed to being property. The next bit of news was that there would be no more bitter Canadian winters for any of them, not that New York winters were much warmer. Fortunately, her close friend Thomas Garrett had all of them well supplied with warm winter clothing.

Harriet returned from St. Catherines to Auburn, New York, with her joyous parents and settled them in her new home—their new home. Even though Harriet was now established in Auburn, her forays to Canada and Maryland to rescue the enslaved did not end. But her life shifted in a new direction when she made that trip to Boston, Massachusetts.

Before Harriet traveled to new places where she would be introduced to unfamiliar individuals, she was known to carry letters of introduction, even though she had remained illiterate. As an added security measure, she had a new photographic invention portraying her friends on her person to show these individuals. Only if they were correctly recognized was her safety assured. Naturally, not all were familiar with the photographic process of the daguerreotype. It had been developed by a French romantic painter, Louis-Jacques-Mandé Daguerre, around 1839. It allowed the photographer to capture an image of a person or object using a wood box, with a lens at one end that threw an image onto a frosted sheet of glass at the other end.

The image was then transferred to highly polished silver-plated sheets of copper, using iodine vapors, developed in mercury fumes and stabilized (or fixed) with salt water or sodium thiosulfate.

Harriet felt entirely at ease carrying both forms of security. If the individual she was to meet did not recognize her friends, she instantly knew not to trust them, left their presence, and quickly moved on.

17

JOHN BROWN

Harriet was not traveling to Boston for pleasure. She was there to fundraise. While in Boston, she had the pleasure of meeting John Brown for a second time. He had become well known for his anti-slavery activism and his fiery speeches wherever he traveled. His deep respect for Harriet had grown as word of her rescue abilities had spread widely, and even though most people fondly referred to her as Moses, since their first meeting up in St. Catherines, John preferred to call her General Tubman. He believed she could command those around her to achieve the desired results and considered her the bravest person he had ever met, man or woman. On their first meeting, they briefly discussed what John Brown believed would be the death blow to American slavery. His plans had further developed and taken shape after Harriet moved to Auburn. Later, she visited Boston to work toward paying Senator William Seward's debt.

John Brown had actively fought slavery in Kansas, along with his sons and other abolitionists, where he gained attention from other supporters as far away as Boston. He also received an invitation from George Stearns, another well-known abolitionist, to meet in Boston with others of the same mindset, a group named the Secret Six. John gratefully accepted the invitation and stopped in New York on the way to Boston, where he met Frederick Douglass, who fondly referred to him, in sympathy, as a Black man. Douglass then brought Harriet and Brown together on that Boston trip. Brown was in Boston to raise money for his fight against slavery as well.

At dinner, Stearns was taken with John Brown's passion for the anti-slavery cause and intended to give John the full support of the Secret Six. His wife, Mary, was far more impressed with Brown's abolition activity and wanted to do whatever it took to raise as much as possible to support him in his endeavors. While the group was taking their time contemplating their support for John, he returned to Kansas to persist in his fight, promising to travel back to Boston shortly.

John met with the other members of the Secret Six upon his return to Boston in the early summer of 1859, as did Harriet, who by now was quite familiar with the entire clandestine group. John was somewhat above board with the group regarding his plans to attack the federal arsenal. The Secret Six gave him rifles and pikes, and Stearns even gifted him his Bowie knife. They knew and believed these were men who were willing to die in the fight to abolish slavery once and for all. They counted on Harriet, who was the most familiar with the lay of the land, to navigate both the approach to and the area surrounding Harpers Ferry, Virginia, where the federal armory was located. The fact that Harriet could neither read nor write was immaterial; she had committed to memory the entire landscape with such precision that John could map out points of attack for his army. Everything on paper indicated it would be a complete success. John planned to capture the weapons from the arsenal and have his army use them, as well as the small number of arms supplied by the Secret Six, to fight the enemy.

In one meeting between Frederick Douglass and John Brown, Frederick told John he was walking into a steel trap. John appealed to Frederick to go with him in what he was convinced would open a mass slave migration through the Appalachian Mountain chain, ending slavery once and for all. Douglass refused to join the mission with John.

On October 16, 1859, with the assistance of only twenty-one men, John attacked the Harpers Ferry Armory in Virginia. He intended to steal nearly ten thousand rifles and muskets to arm local enslaved people, the result being a complete rebellion ending slavery in the United States. They had hidden for three months at a Maryland farm, and once John gave the orders, he and his men marched five miles to Harpers Ferry. Their initial encounter was with the Baltimore and Ohio Railroad Bridge watchman, whom they seized. They successfully captured the musket factory without firing shots; everything was going according to plan. However, the meticulous plan John had put together slowly began to fall apart. The bridge watchman escaped, and he alerted a passing Baltimore and Ohio train. A formerly enslaved person named Heyward Shepherd, who worked as a baggage porter, thought it odd the train was stopping when it shouldn't have been and went to investigate. John's men shot Shepherd, fatally wounding him. The ringing gunshots awakened Dr. John Starry, who ran to Shepherd's side to save him. Brown's men failed to hold the doctor, who ran to the nearby livery, grabbed a horse, and rode to nearby Charles Town, alerting the townspeople of the Ferry seizure.

It was close to dawn when the church and fire bells rang out, awakening roughly ninety well-trained, armed members of the Jefferson Guards militia. They stood in formation in front of the courthouse, and twelve hours after John had initiated his raid, the Jefferson Guards cut off all escape routes, ending his plot. John was trapped in the armory's fire engine house, which he had used as his headquarters. A standoff ensued.

John held townspeople, armory officials, and locals as bargaining chips while he did his best to negotiate. Some of his raiders carried truce flags and were either shot or seized. Even the town mayor was caught up in the curiosity of it all and wandered too close to the engine house; he ended up being fatally shot. Tempers flared as some townspeople killed captive raiders and threatened lynchings while John's forces dwindled. It did not take long until only four raiders, including John, remained.

By midnight on October 17, 1859, eighty-seven US Marines under the command of Lt. Col. Robert E. Lee were dispatched from the Washington Navy Yard. They arrived by train with a planned assault on the fire engine house. The Marines had decided to use bayonets in place of bullets to avoid harming the hostages. They also decided to wait until dawn. John refused to surrender, leaving the Marines no choice but to smash through the door with a sledgehammer. They made a hole large enough for one of them to crawl through, and within a few minutes, John was wounded, the hostages were freed, and the remaining raiders were either killed or captured.

John Brown was seriously injured and captured. He was tried one week later in Charles Town and convicted of murder, treason, and inciting a slave rebellion. On December 2, 1859, he was sentenced to death. Before his hanging, he wrote on a piece of paper his final words, which were handed to the guard and preserved: "I, John Brown, am now quite certain that the crimes of this guilty land will never be purged away but with blood."

Years before John's death, Harriet had experienced repetitive, disturbing dreams that she could not interpret. Typically, since she had received her severe head injury as a young girl, they would reveal their meanings to her—but not this time. When she initially met John Brown, she had recognized him as a significant part of her dream; however, she had not fully comprehended the significance. When the raid at Harpers Ferry occurred, she was in New York and felt the warning signal in her belly that something was amiss. The next day, the news came of the tragedy at Harpers Ferry and the execution of her friend, the courageous John Brown.

John Brown

18

POST-JOHN BROWN

After John's execution, Harriet fell ill and convalesced at the Boston home of Ednah Dow Cheney, a known abolitionist, writer, and philosopher with whom she had become close. Harriet was grateful for Ednah's company as she mourned the loss of John Brown. Not only had Harriet been assisting the Secret Six with valuable information in Boston but she was also fundraising. During the time she spent in Boston giving talks, Harriet raised enough to repay the Sewards for their generous loan to pay for her home, plus additional money to assist fugitives with their resettlement in Auburn until they were able to find housing and viable employment in the area.

John Brown's belief that Harpers Ferry would ignite an uprising that would lead to the end of slavery had not come to pass. But it increased the animosity and tension between those who believed in slavery and those who did not.

Frederick Douglass had initially planned to be at Harpers Ferry with Harriet and the rest of the Secret Six. He, too, was a close friend of Ednah's, traveling in the same abolitionist circles, speaking and writing regularly against slavery. Frederick had been much more fortunate than

Harriet because his enslaver had taught him to read and write. Frederick had initially met Harriet when she brought numerous runaways to his home in Rochester, New York, on their way to Canada. Even though he and Harriet did not cross paths too often, Frederick knew her exhaustive escapee rescue work well. He also believed without a doubt that both would have been killed had they participated in the raid.

After the execution of John Brown, Harriet persisted with her travels back and forth between Auburn and Boston, giving explicit and graphic speeches on the horrors of slavery and how she had managed to shepherd the fleeing enslaved along the extensive Underground Railroad. The more she spoke about fighting for abolition and the importance of women's rights, alongside Ednah Dow Cheney, William Lloyd Garrison, Frederick Douglass, and many others, the more in demand she became. The fact that she was illiterate was a moot point; what she had personally experienced, witnessed, and survived stood out to her audiences. The powerful truth of her rescues and the strength of her oratory drew people to her despite the danger she took upon herself by becoming a public figure. Anyone who heard Harriet speak left deeply inspired and wanting more.

With the passage of the Fugitive Slave Act, Harriet was once again at high risk of being captured and returned to her enslaver. Despite this knowledge, on one trip to Troy, New York, disguised as an older woman, she intervened in the arrest of an enslaved person, Charles Nalle. Even though the marshals had him in custody, Harriet used the enormous crowd as a diversion to get him to freedom, finding a sympathetic boat captain who ferried them both across the river before the marshals could catch up. They managed to disappear in the crushing onslaught of the crowds on the opposite bank. Unfortunately, Nalle was rearrested, and the marshals were alerted via a new invention—the telegraph. Undaunted, Harriet and other crowd members raised enough funds to purchase his freedom. Once he was out of jail, she ensured he and his family safely made it to Schenectady, New York.

The following month, William Seward returned from his travels abroad, and having made a bid for president, he lost the nomination to Abraham Lincoln. Later that year, Seward accepted Lincoln's offer to serve as his secretary of state. No one could have imagined how quickly things would unravel, nor how invaluable the friendship forged between Harriet and the Sewards would become.

19

PRE-CIVIL WAR
AND LINCOLN

Harriet's friend William Lloyd Garrison—who had dubbed her "Moses"—also fondly referred to Harriet as his foster sister. He was one of her biggest promotors on the Boston women's rights speech circuit via his paper, *The Liberator*. Harriet introduced herself as Moses to keep a low profile, especially as things heated up between the North and South. Her friend Ednah Dow Cheney spoke of her heroic endeavors with the Underground Railroad and the many lives Harriet was credited with saving, including those of her parents and siblings. Harriet did not slow her speaking engagements; she remained in high demand, and it was a significant means of support for her and her ailing parents, even as civil war grew increasingly inevitable. Garrison was as fierce an abolitionist as he was a fighter for women's rights, and even with the unrest in the country, he willingly wrote his blistering anti-slavery articles, regardless of the dire threats to his personal safety. He recognized his ability to be a voice for both and fully intended to use it.

Abraham Lincoln

The nation was coming apart at the seams when Abraham Lincoln took the oath of the president of the United States in March 1861. The enormous task of uniting a country torn between ideologies lay before him: those who were pro-slavery and the abolitionists, who had grown in strength and numbers, led by both powerful Black and White voices. Among those were Harriet Tubman, Frederick Douglass, William Seward (President Lincoln's secretary of state), his wife, Frances, and many others. Gathering freed and escaped fugitives resulting from Harriet's sacrifices was no easy task, and that's where Frederick's oratorical skills proved invaluable, as well as Harriet's exceptional skills in delivering speeches. Many enslaved people were cautious of President Lincoln—and with good reason. Could the president be trusted to free all the slaves throughout the entire country—or only in the North? What would occur if he were given a second term? Too many enslaved had watched their family members needlessly suffer at the hands of brutal, merciless slaveholders. Others had held out hope while their loved ones had gone off to war to fight against the Confederacy, only to be paid less money than their White counterparts. They wondered if Lincoln could be president to everyone. Frederick Douglass knew it was time to speak with his one-time foe, President Abraham Lincoln, and determine where he stood prior to the election, to assuage his people. He went to the White House optimistically inclined to trust the re-elected president but was nearly turned away because he was a Black man. Frederick needed to know where President Lincoln stood on the issue of freeing all the slaves. He finally spoke with him and left content that they were now friends. He couldn't have known then that this would be the last time he would speak to him. Several days later, he heard Lincoln's speech on the White House lawn and knew the president had listened to his words.

A month following Lincoln's inauguration, the boiling point occurred, on April 12, 1861, when the Confederates fired the first shots over Fort Sumter, South Carolina, after President Lincoln issued an order to resupply the fort using a fleet of ships. Southerners had planned to revolt since Lincoln's election, and the Northern abolitionists had been readying for the inevitable; thus far, seven states had already seceded from the country.

After two days of fierce bombardment by the Confederates, Fort Sumter's Union commander, Major Robert Anderson, surrendered to the Confederate Army, led by General Pierre G. T. Beauregard. One Union death and two Union casualties were due to a cannon misfire.

In mid-1861, Harriet Tubman was recruited as part of the Massachusetts military attachment at Fort Monroe, on the Chesapeake Bay in Virginia, under the command of General Benjamin Butler. Her volunteer duties as the only Black individual included cooking and laundry. As the fort was flooded with families and children, she was frequently called on to act as a nurse. Harriet had been a caretaker since she was a child on the plantation, so caring for others was second nature. Harriet remained there for approximately four months, long enough to see many individuals endure hard, unpaid manual work, such as building roads and dikes, making many of them wonder if they had switched masters. The consensus was that the war would not last more than a few months as the Northern states' population was roughly twenty million, and the South's population was nine million.

Patriotism was euphoric; filling volunteer quotas was a simple task. With the issuance of Lincoln's proclamation and the calling up of militia, volunteers lined up in droves with thousands of men enthusiastic to risk their lives to save the Union. Harriet was more than willing to do her part, having risked her life to save the lives of enslaved people well before the first shots of the war were fired. Now was her time to use her skill set for the wartime effort and help the Union to victory.

20

CIVIL WAR SCOUT

Harriet Tubman's notoriety had spread far and wide years before the first shots on Fort Sumter, so it was no surprise President Lincoln and the Union Army generals knew of her. Even though she had served well in her brief stint at Fort Monroe, they had more specific, in-depth plans for Harriet. No one else in the Union Army had Harriet's familiarity with the Deep South, which she could apply in daylight or at night. No one was as innately skilled in either disguises or evasive maneuvers as Harriet. She was as natural a fit as any spy or scout for the Union Army and was more expertly trained than any soldier they currently had in uniform—regardless of rank—having traversed the terrain more than several times on foot.

The extreme seasonal weather conditions had no consequence for Harriet. She led fugitives to safety through heavy snowstorms and drifts that blocked bounty hunters as they attempted to cross into northern territory. Her assailants were unable to keep up with her in the southern summer heat, nor in the cooler night air. Not even the lifelong effects of her traumatic head injury slowed her down. The generals knew she was a force to be reckoned with and were beyond grateful she was on their side. Another of Harriet's invaluable military assets was her innate ability to control her facial expressions, enabling her to act out whatever character was necessary, whenever it was called upon, at a moment's notice. For example, if she were stopped and questioned, she would pretend to be entirely stupid and convince her interrogator that she could not comprehend what was being asked of her and, therefore, be left alone and free to go about her business.

Not only were President Lincoln and the generals aware of Harriet's exploits and growing legend, but so was the governor of Massachusetts, John A. Andrew, who passionately assisted her whenever she needed help. The major problem in the latter part of 1861, as Union troops overtook parts of South Carolina, Georgia, and Florida, was that White plantation owners fled, leaving behind approximately ten thousand enslaved people with no place to go other than the Union camps. They had limited clothing and no food. The encampments found themselves overrun by thousands of people in a desperate situation without assistance—no jobs, no education, and no prospects. Governor Andrew requested Harriet's aid and assigned her to General David Hunter. Out of gratitude for all she had done to rescue enslaved people and in recognition of her talents, General Hunter—the Union commander of the Department of the South—issued her an invaluable military pass that read, "Give her free passage at all times on all government transports. Harriet Tubman is a valuable woman. As a government servant, she can purchase such provisions from the Commissary as needed."

Once at Fort Mitchell, on Hilton Head Island, South Carolina, Harriet's work as a spy and scout began in earnest. Before engaging in assignments, Harriet's initial mission was to settle the now-freed people and help them establish a future. Her initial unexpected hurdle was a language barrier; they either spoke a mix of English and their native African tongue or Gullah, an unfamiliar Creole language. They laughed at her accent when she attempted to explain things to them. Her instinctive good nature carried her through the rough spots as they worked side by side, and their mutual trust slowly began to build. The bonds grew stronger as Harriet shared her small food rations from the commissary with them, baking pies and making root beer to sell to the soldiers. She enlisted their aid in the sales of the goods to the soldiers. Harriet also opened a washhouse and hired them as necessary workers. Everyone, including the soldiers, benefited from Harriet's efforts over the following year. The bond strengthened between the formerly enslaved and Harriet. They had enough confidence in her to share vital information with her regarding the unfamiliar region.

Harriet formed a close-knit group of highly trusted scouts who meticulously mapped out the nearby territory for her, including the interconnecting local waterways. She had great faith in her handpicked crew but did not let on that she was completely illiterate. Harriet, in turn, paid them for their diligence with the money General Hunter had given her. She was also able to do some personal scouting of the area they were planning to infiltrate. The exact locations of Confederate troops, and especially their ordnance, were imperative to the success of the upcoming mission entrusted to her by General David Hunter. The more Harriet memorized about the land, the greater her ability to protect her scouts, who had become like family. The mission depended on her not missing any detail, even if it seemed trivial or insignificant. Nothing could be left to chance; too many lives depended on the successful infiltration.

While still based at Fort Mitchell, Harriet was briefly called away to Port Royal in South Carolina to join Dr. Henry K. Durand, the director of the freedman's hospital. Once again, her renown in the healing arts area preceded her and was desperately required. Soldiers, as well as fugitives, were dying from a variety of diseases, including typhoid, cholera, malaria, dysentery, yellow fever, and chicken pox. Harriet was known to have used roots as natural remedies before she was a conductor on the Underground Railroad and to have cured many of her patients suffering from ailments. According to Sarah Bradford Hopkins's Tubman biography, *Moses of Her People*—in which the author directly interviewed her subject—herbal healing knowledge had been passed to Harriet from her mother. Rit had taught Harriet how to boil cranesbill and lily roots to make a bitter-tasting tea. It was used to treat fevers, smallpox, and other infectious diseases. Everything she knew had been passed down through her family, beginning with her grandmother, Modesty. Harriet was honored to help mend the ailing Union soldiers and fugitives, and her legend grew.

Harriet Tubman Knowlton Award

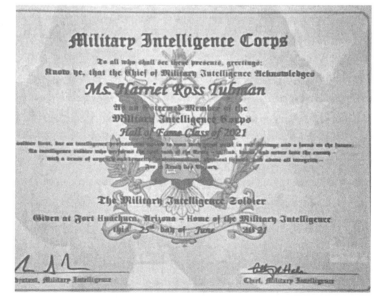

Harriet Tubman Military Intelligence Certificate

21

COMBAHEE RIVER RAID

The Spaniards first came to the Combahee River in South Carolina in 1520 and were under the impression that they had discovered it. Vasque de Ayllon initially named it the River Jordan. It was subsequently renamed the Combahee after its first inhabitants, the Combahee tribe of Native Americans. The stream would eventually become a true River Jordan for potentially more than 750 enslaved Africans who, under the combined leadership of Harriet Tubman and Colonel James Montgomery, would finally be delivered.

More than three centuries after de Ayllon, in the latter part of 1862, General David Hunter was authorized by President Abraham Lincoln to form two Black regiments in South Carolina, made up of freedmen. Being the commander of the Department of the South, he ordered General James Montgomery, another familiar abolitionist, to take command of the second regiment—the Second South Carolina Infantry—and General Thomas Wentworth Higginson, also a fellow abolitionist, to be commander of the first regiment—the First South Carolina Infantry.

When the prospect of embarking on the Combahee River Raid came to fruition and was no longer in the mission training stages, General Hunter approached Harriet, trusting in her judgment to make the best choice of whom she felt most comfortable leading the raid. She did not take too long to decide. She was fully aware of General Montgomery's stature as an activist and his respected leadership of the second regiment. Having personally spent an extended period with his scouts, examining enemy posts and comprehending the depth of the dangers of the mission at hand, Harriet requested General James Montgomery lead it. General Montgomery had been one of John Brown's men, and Harriet was well acquainted with him. General Hunter agreed with Harriet that General Montgomery would be the best fit. They immediately set about drawing up plans for the raid, the success of which depended almost entirely on the information Harriet and her scouts had gathered in the last few months, putting many lives at risk.

Harriet and her team of scouts had traveled, by foot and boat, up and down the Combahee River, combing the riverbanks, quietly engaging with many enslaved people who knew where the Confederates had placed river mines. The maps of the mine placements were drawn from Harriet's photographic memory, which later proved to be 100 percent accurate.

The Confederates anticipated an eventual waterway attack, coupled with a land assault, and were outnumbered, so they needed every possible advantage. They had not counted on Harriet Tubman gaining the trust and confidence of the enslaved with promises and guarantees of freedom if they aided her and her covert band of Black spies in discovering the underwater locations of the mines. The enslaved people had been forced to place the mines, so they knew the location of each one. Harriet would sail down the river, go to each slave cabin, locate the enslaved people who had placed the mines, and enlist their help in deactivating the mines. With the offer of freedom, Harriet felt she could count on them in her heart. Harriet also knew her promise was not an empty one. She would get her people out of Egypt. The difference for Harriet in this instance was that this was not her Egypt. She was in unfamiliar territory. She did not speak the language as she did on the Eastern Shore. She had built up confidence and trust with the band of Gullah-speaking spies and scouts she had worked with for some time. The trust she had earned from Port Royal carried over here;

word had traveled, and they believed Harriet would keep her promise and help them to a better life.

Statue of Harriet Tubman in Beaufort, South Carolina

June 2, 1863: The night was chosen by General James Montgomery to set sail from Beaufort, South Carolina, with Harriet Tubman at his side, aboard the lead gunboat, the *John Adams*. Accompanied by additional gunboats, which were retrofitted paddlewheel boats—the *Sentinel* and the *Harriet A. Weed*—they would initiate the raid on the Confederate strongholds. Due to her and the team's proficient scouting, the general knew where the enemy torpedoes and floating mines had been placed and gave specific orders for the exact routes to follow. Under his command, the gunboat's safety was further ensured, knowing the mines had been defused and removed by the enslaved people and the charts had been marked accordingly.

The mission was two-pronged: the Union soldiers were there to attack and destroy as many enemy supply depots as possible, including any buildings or estates holding weapons or artillery for the Confederate troops, and to rescue as many enslaved people as possible. Montgomery further instructed his troops, as they quickly went to shore, to disperse the Confederate sentinels at Fields Point, a fortified peninsula on high ground overlooking the Combahee River. The soldiers burned the surrounding plantations, bridges, rice mills, cotton, corn, potatoes, and storehouses—whatever could not be seized was burned. The destruction continued throughout the night while Harriet guided the boats as close to the riverbanks as was safe. Although there was a bit of chaos as rowboats approached the shore to transport the escapees to the waiting boats, Harriet is said to have sung familiar songs from the ship's deck to calm nerves.

While the necessary destruction of fields and supplies continued, the gunboats sounded their whistles; Harriet had notified the enslaved people to await this signal. She had instructed them to be prepared for it, gather what they could, and run for the riverbanks; this was where they would discover their first bit of freedom. More than seven hundred men, women, and children responded that night, some with chickens and pigs. In speeches years later, Harriet recalled this moment and once again made the analogy to the people fleeing Egypt.

The Union troops were not destroying arbitrary plantations; they had been given specific orders to utterly pillage and burn properties that leading South Carolinian secessionists owned. The secessionists included the Heyward, Middleton, and Lowndes families, considered part of the ruling class by many formerly enslaved people serving as Union soldiers. Those soldiers took great personal pleasure in the destruction of their former masters' plantations, crops, and other property.

The bulk of the damage had been done by the time the Confederate troops became aware of the Union attack. A company of Confederates was sent to thwart the remaining attack by firing on the Union gunboats, but they missed and were unsuccessful.

The raid proved an enormous military success for the Union, having cut off a significant supply-shipping source for the Confederates. It opened a vital river artery for the Union to protect its interests. As a bonus, General Montgomery gained close to two hundred recruits due to the bravery of Harriet and her team. It was the first and only time in the Civil War that a woman played a pivotal role in planning and carrying out strategic military operations.

The Emancipation Proclamation Act, permitting Black soldiers to sign up to fight for the Union, had been in effect since January 1, 1863. Many doubted their bravery until their masterful efforts in the Combahee River Raid encouraged thousands of freed Black men to enlist in the Union Army.

Franklin B. Sanborn, a Boston newspaper journalist for the *Commonwealth*, who reported on the Combahee River Raid in July of 1863, described the event as "a gallant band of Black soldiers, under the guidance of a Black woman, dashed into the enemy's country, struck a bold and effective blow, destroying millions of dollars' worth of commissary stores, cotton, and lordly dwellings, and striking terror into the heart of rebeldom . . . without losing a man or receiving a scratch. It was a glorious consummation." He identified Harriet Tubman one month later as "the Black woman," introducing her as a spy for all to know and putting her in the spotlight for the first time. The *Commonwealth* was a well-known anti-slavery paper in Boston, and Sanborn justified giving her credit for a successful mission. She had once again put her life on the line to save others, this time in the name of the Union Army.

Following the Combahee River Raid, several generals requested that Harriet remain in the South for as long as necessary because of her extraordinary abilities as a scout and a spy. General Hunter agreed, as she had proven her exceptional intelligence skills. Even though Harriet was called upon now and then for spy and scout missions, her war duties after the raid were more typical of women supporting the Union efforts. She mentored newly freed enslaved people as they sought paid labor using basic skills, such as baking and selling pies, and she passed on extensive farming knowledge.

Approximately a month and a half after the Combahee raid, she took on a new assignment, helping serve meals to the men of the Massachusetts Fifty-Fourth Regiment—one of the first Black regiments—led by Colonel Robert Gould Shaw. Colonel Shaw fought hard for equal pay for his men when he became aware that they were receiving less than White soldiers. Unfortunately, Colonel Robert Shaw did not live to see the passage of equal pay for all soldiers, regardless of color, by Congress in June of 1864. The bill pertained to those men who had been free since April 19, 1861.

Harriet witnessed the fierce assault on the Confederate-held Fort Wagner, led by Colonel Shaw. She wondered which among the brave Fifty-Fourth Regiment soldiers she had served breakfast to were still alive as she heard thunderous guns fired on them. When the battle finally ended, the survivors gathered and counted the horrendous casualties. Colonel Shaw's body was held by Confederate General Johnson Hagood as retribution and buried in a trench with his deceased soldiers.

The wounded Union soldiers were segregated, and the White ones were sent to Hilton Head under the care of White nurse Clara Barton, the future founder of the Red Cross. The Black soldiers of the Fifty-Fourth remained in Beaufort under the care of Harriet Tubman, who used all her natural healing knowledge to tend to the men's varying wounds.

22

FINALLY, A FURLOUGH

On her way home by train, in June of 1864, to see her parents in Auburn, New York, Harriet attempted to recall how much time had elapsed since she last saw them. While she was trying to add up the years, the faces of the young men she had treated passed before her mind's eye. Many had survived thanks to her, while others had died regardless of what she did. She comforted all of them with her singing and remained until the end with those who didn't make it. She was their nurse and healer, as well as a military woman.

Harriet spent time unwinding with her parents, Rit and Ben, and enjoyed breathing in fresh air without artillery shells before traveling to Boston to meet with her abolitionist friends. Her life consisted of never-ending work for abolition even though the Emancipation Proclamation had passed. It was a known fact that Black soldiers whom Confederate soldiers captured were sold into slavery in Texas or other Southern states where the Proclamation Act was either not recognized or ignored. The Black soldiers were sometimes tortured and then executed, or just the latter. Lincoln had persistently pushed and encouraged border states to amend their state constitutions to abolish slavery. In Harriet's mind, a tremendous amount of work lay ahead of her, and as much as she wanted to spend time with her parents, she felt an urgent call to go to Boston.

In early August, while in Boston, Harriet stayed at the home of John S. Rock, a freeborn Black man and well-known abolitionist. He was one of the first Black men in the country to receive his medical license. John introduced Harriet to Sojourner Truth, an abolitionist of great stature.

Sojourner was born into slavery in New York around 1798 with the name Isabella. She escaped in 1826 with the help of Quaker abolitionists. She became a street corner evangelist and founded a shelter for homeless women. When someone asked her name during her travels, she replied, "Sojourner." She was a citizen of heaven and a wanderer on earth. She adopted the surname Truth, meaning that God was her Father and His name was Truth. She went on to become a women's rights advocate and lecturer. Like Harriet, Sojourner worked during the Civil War, and she performed similar duties, such as nursing and cooking. Now, they needed to collaborate with other abolitionists for an ongoing cause. Like Harriet, Sojourner gave many speeches throughout her life, her most famous being "Ain't I a Woman?" in response to a man arguing against the right of women to vote.

Unlike Sojourner, Harriet had not met President Lincoln; she had only been introduced to Mary Todd Lincoln. Harriet held a school of thought comparable to Frederick Douglass's in that she was somewhat skeptical of the president. Unlike Frederick Douglass, Harriet's line of thinking did not change toward Lincoln until after he had passed and she learned more about him from Frederick Douglass. Had it not been for the influence of Frederick Douglass, Black soldiers may not have fought alongside White soldiers nor eventually received equal pay. Like Douglass and Colonel Shaw of the Fifty-Fourth regiment, Sojourner and Harriet held strong feelings regarding equal pay for Black soldiers.

Harriet left Boston to return to a hospital near Fort Monroe, as the Union Army once again required her services to tend to the health and well-being of the soldiers.

23

SURRENDER AND THE FIRST JUNETEENTH

On April 9, 1865, General Robert E. Lee surrendered at Appomattox Court House to General Ulysses S. Grant. Harriet was asked to come to Fort Monroe in Virginia, even though the Civil War had concluded, under the command of General Benjamin F. Butler. Despite the various proclamations, word regarding the end of slavery had not made its way to Texas, which meant enslaved people continued to remain under the control of their masters as if nothing had changed.

Harriet's funds began to run low, especially since the US Army was no longer paying her for her services and she had to support her parents. She worried about their ability to keep a roof over their heads and how she could assist those who had come to her for refuge until they found employment. Harriet had to set aside her financial fears, as she had always done, and focus on her work; but her parents depended on her. Somehow, she would find a way.

Before performing her final duties at Fort Monroe, Virginia, she continued to care for the war-wounded and visited the surgeon general, William Hammond, in Washington, DC. Harriet believed she had to make sure the surgeon general was aware of the harsh conditions faced by the Black soldiers she had cared for.

Texas did its level best to hold on to the viewpoint that the Emancipation Proclamation did not apply to them, since they were a territory rather than a formal state. Many enslavers had intentionally moved there to find a haven for their enslavement beliefs. They claimed the enslaved people were needed for their harvest and, as such, insisted they had a right to withhold legal information from them for as long as deemed necessary. Texans further claimed that there was a severe labor shortage and without the enslaved people, they would lose their crops, devastating their economy. Union soldiers, led by General Gordon Granger, refused to indulge them. His troops arrived in full force in Galveston that June, announcing that all approximately 250,000 enslaved were now free—hence, Juneteenth Day.

In June of that same year, Harriet made the arduous trip home to Auburn, New York, for the last time as the Civil War finally concluded. Another battle for her was only beginning: to obtain monetary compensation for all she had willingly given to the Union. She needed to be recognized as the first woman in the country's history to have ever led a military raid, in addition to being a spy, a scout, and a nurse.

24

A NEW CHAPTER BEGINS

Harriet made her last war-related return home to Auburn, New York, when she was approximately fifty years of age, surrounded by her family and friends after four long years of battle and caring for sick, injured, and dying soldiers. It was the beginning of a new life for all of them, especially with the passage of the Emancipation Proclamation. With the Fugitive Slave Act no longer in force, they were all free to go wherever they pleased, without fear of reprisal from either slave patrols or bounty hunters. There remained the matter of her collecting money from the Union Army for services performed during those years, her work being equal to that of any other soldier who had served.

Harriet deposited her paltry earnings at the local bank in Auburn. She collected enough from boarders at her Auburn home and wages from housecleaning, selling produce, raising pigs, and selling baked goods to make a decent living to provide for herself and her parents. As a regular bank customer, she became good friends with banker Charles P. Wood. He was aware of her prestigious reputation during the war. Mr. Wood offered to prepare a detailed account of Harriet's war service and military record to present to Congress, free of charge, hoping she would be paid for services rendered.

In addition to his role as a banker, Wood was well known in Auburn for his outstanding contributions to the war effort. He had seen to it that the first locally recruited troops wore far improved uniforms over what had initially been disbursed. When military men perished in the war, Charles ensured that their families did not suffer financially, and he did whatever he could to provide relief. Therefore, it shouldn't be surprising that he stepped up and provided his services to Harriet.

Wood meticulously outlined Harriet's war contributions—her work as a spy, a scout, and a nurse. He spoke at length with Harriet to ensure accuracy in all his illustrative bullet points. Wood knew everything on paper had to be authenticated and adequately prepared for congressional approval for Harriet to qualify for her pension. Everything had gone through proper channels—including General Clinton MacDougal, now a local congressman—and all the boxes were correctly checked.

Unfortunately, nothing could have prepared Wood—or anyone else—for the backlog of bills awaiting Congress, which had accumulated because of the end of the war and the ensuing Reconstruction period. There was an order of priority, and a Black woman was at the very end of the line—far behind states' rights and war pensions for White men. Due to the suffragettes' hard work, women's rights had also recently landed on the table. Harriet would have to be patient and wait, even though she had the accomplishments and name recognition to back up her financial claims. Congress pointed to a lack of written army records as their official reason for the preliminary denial.

Harriet remained optimistic that the document Mr. Wood had diligently worked on would eventually reach the appropriate desk. No one could have predicted how long approval would take or that it would ultimately require a congressional bill for Harriet to receive her due compensation. In the interim, she needed to solve the other issues in front of her.

Harriet believed in helping as many people as possible, even if it left her short on money, a situation that occurred throughout her lifetime. She was satisfied if she had sufficient funds left over to support her parents. She believed that she would be provided for if she did her best.

To supplement Wood's efforts, Harriet also engaged her longtime friend Secretary of State William Seward to help her effort to receive compensation. Shockingly, on April 15, 1865—just a few days after the South surrendered—President Abraham Lincoln was assassinated at Ford's Theatre in Washington, DC. William Seward was also a victim of the conspiracy, as a former Confederate soldier attacked him in his home while Lincoln was at the playhouse. Seward received stab wounds to the face and neck. He managed to survive, but his recovery took several weeks. With the country in turmoil, it would be some time before Harriet's financial situation would be addressed.

Meanwhile, shortly after returning home from the war, a veteran named Nelson Davis arrived from Elizabeth City, North Carolina, and appeared on Harriet's doorstep. He had been told to go to town, where he might find a spare room for rent, meals included. Like Harriet, he had escaped slavery in Maryland. He was several years her junior and had learned the brickmaking trade before becoming a soldier. His ability to find work in Auburn meant he was a paying boarder, whereas many others were not. The money was exceptionally helpful in maintaining a roof over everyone's heads. Nelson was also happy to pitch in if anything around the house needed repair.

Having Nelson under the same roof greatly benefited Harriet, not just because he added to the financial coffers and performed services. He and Harriet knew what was in each other's hearts, as they had both been enslaved. They had both exhibited bravery in running for their freedom and in their respective fights for the Union Army. They had both witnessed the spectacle and horrors of slavery and war. They formed a unique connection and friendship that grew over time, and Harriet treasured it.

Yet Harriet refused to let go of the hope that the army would financially compensate her for her years of military service. While she bided her time, she found another project to hold her attention: neighbors and other Auburn citizens had enlisted the aid of a noted historical author, Sarah Bradford, to help spread her message and support her effort.

Sarah interviewed Harriet at length for a biography: *Scenes in the Life of Harriet Tubman*. The book's printing was financed by Harriet's close, dependable friends Gerrit Smith, Wendell Phillips, and William Seward, as well as numerous others who supported her cause. The book sales raised an estimated $1,200 for a financially struggling Harriet, and although it fell far short of being equivalent to her war contributions, it was sufficient to smooth the proverbial financial waters temporarily.

25

THE SUFFRAGETTE ERA

Harriet's long-term friendship with Lucretia Mott, which stemmed from her Underground Railroad days, led her to a new pathway after the end of the Civil War—the suffrage movement, a cause supported and organized by both Black and White women. Through her connection with Mott, she met others in the women's movement. She became sympathetic to the cause and eager to be part of it. Harriet staunchly believed in equal rights for all people—Black or White, male or female. However, the National Women's Suffrage Association, begun by Susan B. Anthony and Elizabeth Cady Stanton in May of 1869, opposed the Fifteenth Amendment because it granted the right to vote to Black men but not to women, regardless of color.

Harriet preferred the role of supporter rather than being in the limelight as a leader. But she was perfectly suited to being a speaker, according to Lucretia. As a result, Harriet made frequent trips to Boston, delivering speeches that illustrated her experiences escaping slavery, rescuing others, and eventually becoming a remarkable military spy, scout, and nurse—and yet she could not vote. Her story astonished one audience after the other, and the demand to hear Moses spread. She toured from New York to Washington in support of women's rights. Harriet's money from her speaking fees was substantial enough for the upkeep of her Auburn home and ongoing care for her aging parents. She felt at ease traveling and leaving her home in the capable hands of Nelson, who continued to oversee repairs regardless of the season.

Harriet Tubman residence on South Avenue in Fleming, New York, next to Auburn

Fortunately, she was a welcome guest among fellow equal rights activists, war veterans, and suffragettes. Her extensive network of friendships meant that she always had lodging, and payment was never an issue.

At the same time, the first Sarah Bradford biography, *Scenes in the Life of Harriet Tubman*, continued to do well, granting her the financial freedom to work with the suffragettes. No one noticed or remarked that Harriet remained entirely illiterate; they were far too intrigued by her daring tales of one trip after another to rescue enslaved people, regardless of the bounty on her head and the constant danger. It became apparent to everyone who met Harriet that her intelligence was far above the average intelligence level of either men or women, and she had a tremendous breadth of knowledge even without having received a formal education.

When asked how she was able to keep the small children and babies quiet while being endlessly hunted, Harriet admitted that, out of necessity, for survival for all, the children were given small amounts of paregoric, a tincture made of opium. At this point, Harriet would remind her listeners of her nursing background and the Ashanti medicinal heritage she had learned from her mother, which had been passed down from her grandmother, Modesty.

Harriet Tubman

Harriet explained to her audiences that many groups she rescued, including those with small children, moved at night. In the dark stillness of the woods, noises of any kind—especially crying babies—could have been pinpointed from long distances. Harriet would expound on this and convey to her rapt assemblage how frequently the escapees were forced to hide in the underbrush, covered with blankets or sometimes only leaves when bounty hunters were nearby, until it was safe to move on. According to oral family history passed down through generations, Harriet carried a pistol in case any escapees attempted to leave their hiding places. No one has since been able to verify if the gun was loaded, and no records exist to determine whether her escapees were ever shot.

Even though Harriet had experienced a severe head injury as a young girl, it never slowed her speaking schedule. Harriet refused to allow the persistent headaches to prevent her from educating as many as possible about the horrors of slavery, which she and over four million others had endured. She accepted her part as the messenger on behalf of those countless faces who had suffered and perished.

Harriet did not hesitate to answer questions regarding her days as an enslaved person and the workload her masters demanded of her daily. Her workday never ended. She related stories of pulling a wagon—the same function as a horse—to prove her worth to plantation owners. Not only was Harriet expected to plow the fields for planting, but her duties also included keeping up with the "Big House," keeping it entirely dust-free and ensuring her enslavers' children were clean and well fed. If the babies awakened in the middle of the night, it was her responsibility, not the mother's, to run from the slave quarters to tend to them. Typically, a messenger from the Big House would hurry down to the slave quarters and rouse Harriet from sleep.

Harriet imparted to her listeners the gravity of why all people had to come together to lift the rights of African American women, especially those who had been trapped in slavery and, like herself, had little to no education. It explained why they had a limited skill set for any job besides housekeeping or plowing.

Harriet spoke energetically alongside Susan B. Anthony and Elizabeth Cady Stanton as they sought equal rights for women in the workplace and the voting booth. Harriet inspired people at these gatherings to continue fighting with courage and faith.

Another of Harriet's old friends, Frederick Douglass, was also a staunch supporter of Anthony, Stanton, and their suffrage work. Throughout many of his joint talks with them, they knew they could count on his ability to rally the crowds and make passionate speeches whenever he was in the area.

Elizabeth Cady Stanton was born in 1815 and grew up in Johnstown, New York, where she attended the Presbyterian Church. She spent her life traveling and delivering speeches on equal rights. She denounced the clergy for failing to support women's rights.

Elizabeth Cady Stanton

Susan B. Anthony was born in 1820 in Adams, Massachusetts. She delivered speeches in public, even though many people at the time deemed it improper for a woman to do so. No obstacle or authority ever prevented Anthony, Stanton, or Tubman from speaking out in favor of women's rights, including voting rights.

The fight for women's voting rights did not come about easily. Anthony and Stanton formed the first women's suffrage movement, the National

Woman Suffrage Association (NWSA), in 1869. It was specifically in opposition to the Fifteenth Amendment, which enfranchised Black men, still disallowing women of any color the right to vote. In the year following the ratification of the amendment, they sent a voting rights request to both houses of Congress asking that voting rights be extended to women and that their concerns be heard on the floor of Congress.

Susan B. Anthony

A second national suffrage organization was established in 1868: the American Woman Suffrage Association (AWSA), founded by Lucy Stone, Julia Ward Howe, and Thomas Wentworth Higginson. In their opinion, they were less confrontational than the NWSA and felt gaining the women's vote could be accomplished at the local level, thus bringing it to national attention.

The two organizations merged in 1890, becoming the National American Woman Suffrage Association (NAWSA). It was the largest woman suffrage organization in the country, finally accomplishing its goal of ratifying the Nineteenth Amendment, giving women the right to vote, in 1920, long after Harriet Tubman had passed, leaving her mark on the fight for all to remember to this day and beyond.

26

NELSON DAVIS, MARRIAGE, AND AFTERWARD

Harriet and Nelson had numerous things in common before they ever met. Having both escaped slavery and safely made their way north—from Maryland and North Carolina, respectively—they both achieved heroic status for different reasons. Nelson was a quiet hero, having served as a private in Company G in the Eighth United States Colored Regiment from September 1863 to November 1865. Harriet followed the path of a conductor and later became an invaluable military spy, scout, and nurse and, after the war, was a sought-after speaker for women's rights.

Nelson's regiment trained in Philadelphia and was sent to Hilton Head Island. From there, they pushed south to Florida. His unit served with distinction at the Battle of Olustee, to the west of Jacksonville, Florida, and then they were moved back north to Petersburg and Richmond. They were one of the units at General Lee's surrender at Appomattox. Following this event, Nelson's unit was transferred to Texas, where he was honorably discharged in 1865.

There are unsubstantiated claims that Harriet and Nelson met while serving in the military since they may have been in the same place at the same time. However, there is no concrete evidence of this one way or the other. They officially met when Nelson appeared on Harriet's porch, requesting a room to rent in her Auburn, New York, home.

Their relationship was comfortable and grew over time, even with Harriet's frequent absences while she traveled in support of the growing suffragette movement. Harriet was settled and at ease in Nelson's company whenever she was home.

It proved to be a natural step for Harriet and Nelson to marry on March 18, 1869, at the Central Presbyterian Church in Auburn. Nothing stood in the way of the wedding, as her first husband, John Tubman, already estranged, had died several years previously.

Harriet and Nelson's wedding certificate

Following the couple's wedding, Harriet continued her demanding traveling schedule. Although Nelson worked as a brickmaker and had an ongoing stream of boarders, they needed every penny from her speeches, as they were always skirting the edge of poverty. They did whatever was necessary to care for themselves and Harriet's parents, including growing and selling vegetables to neighbors in town.

Harriet Tubman and Nelson Davis

As the years passed, things became more challenging for them as Harriet's parents aged and required more care. Fortunately, several of Harriet's brothers moved into the house and pitched in with caregiving responsibilities.

At the same time, interest in Harriet's speeches intensified rapidly. She was determined to maintain her extraordinary schedule; she felt it was her obligation to relate her story.

A few years after Harriet and Nelson were married, one of the nearest and dearest people to her passed away of old age: her father, Ben, the most gentle man in her life. He had taught her everything she needed regarding celestial navigation—information that had saved her life and countless others' during their treks north. The wisdom he had imparted to her of the waterways instilled in her the knowledge to become the first woman to lead a military river raid, rescuing hundreds of additional people. She would carry his teachings throughout her life. Harriet made sure her father was buried with the utmost respect in Auburn.

Shortly after Ben passed away, in 1871, Harriet suffered the loss of one of her close friends, William Seward. Harriet had been forever grateful to him for providing help to purchase her home, which she had quickly repaid.

This act had allowed her to do more than she had ever dreamt possible as a formerly enslaved person. In Seward's passing, Harriet lost a dear friend and benefactor who believed in her. They had become so close that she considered him family. With both Sewards having passed—Frances died in 1865—she now mourned two of her closest friends.

William Seward

One aspect of pure joy in Harriet's and Nelson's lives was adopting a young girl named Gertie. It remains unknown why Gertie's parents—who had once been enslaved—were unable to continue raising her, but she had certainly come to a warm and loving family in the Tubman-Davis home.

Harriet, Gertie, and Nelson

Harriet had many supporters over the years and developed a trusting nature. It never occurred to her that someone would ever take advantage of her, especially when she had been doing so much to help others. She gave away far more than she kept for herself, always looking out for others in her care.

Portrait of Harriet Tubman at midlife taken by Benjamin F. Powelson

Harriet's vulnerability and the constant battle to avoid poverty made her an easy mark for a scam. As the Union Army advanced deeper into Confederate-held territory, it was common knowledge that slaveholders had ordered their enslaved to bury valuables—paper money included—as deep into the earth as possible on their plantations. They believed they would return when things had blown over to retrieve their belongings.

Harriet didn't seem suspicious when two men approached her and her brother, John Stewart. She proposed giving them $5,000 in gold for less than half that in greenbacks, the currency used during the Civil War.

Harriet privately asked a friend in Auburn for the lesser amount, and he readily agreed. In exchange, she would return the lower amount to him, making it a good investment.

Portrait of Harriet Tubman taken between 1871-1876 by photographer Harvey B. Lindsey

The two men planned the exchange with Harriet, John, and Nelson at night in the woods. The con men were able to separate Harriet from Nelson and John, knocking her down to the ground and running off with the money, leaving Harriet empty-handed.

Harriet refused to be daunted by the incident. Instead, she pressed on, as she had always done. Sadly, before Harriet could go on with her life's plans, she lost another pillar in her life: her mother, Rit, in October 1880. As with her father, Harriet knew that Rit's spirit would continue to guide her.

27

ONWARD WITH THE DREAM

The loss of both parents in a short span wasn't Harriet's only tragedy. Shortly after that, a portion of her wood-frame Auburn home caught fire. Thankfully, there were no injuries to them or their boarders, and Nelson had the perfect skill set to repair the damage, immediately setting about making and firing bricks. He hired local men to reinforce the home with his newly produced bricks. It was sturdier than the earlier wood-frame version and no longer vulnerable to fire. The downside was that it once again left them in a financially tricky condition.

In 1886, a timely opportunity presented itself: Sarah Hopkins Bradford approached Harriet regarding a revised and updated version of *Scenes in the Life of Harriet Tubman*, with a catchier title, *Harriet Tubman, the Moses of Her People*. It had been eighteen years since its publication, and Mrs. Bradford suggested that it would now attract an even broader audience, as Harriet had remained in public life for the nearly two decades since the first book's publication.

Harriet heartily signed on, believing it would significantly improve the family's finances. Additionally, it would allow Harriet to make public letters from various influential people whose paths she had crossed, without whom she would not have had the chance to be a part of the speaking circuit. Harriet and Sarah set about the interview process as soon as Nelson and his men completed work on the house.

Letter from Mr. Oliver John for the second edition:

New York, March 6, 1886
My Dear Madam,

I am happy to learn that you are about to publish a revised edition of your life of that heroic woman, Harriet Tubman, [with] whose assistance so many enslaved Americans were enabled to break their bonds.

During the period of my official connection with the Anti-Slavery office in New York, I saw her frequently, when she came there with the companies of enslaved people, whom she had successfully piloted away from the South; and often listened with wonder to the story of her adventures and hair-breadth escapes.

She always told her tale with a modesty which showed how unconscious she was of having done anything more than her simple duty. No one who listened to her could doubt her perfect truthfulness and integrity.

Her shrewdness in planning the escape of slaves, her skill in avoiding arrest, her courage in every emergency, and her willingness to endure hardship and face any danger for the sake of her poor followers were phenomenal.

I regret to hear that she is poor and ill, and hope the sale of your book will give her the relief she so much needs and so well deserves.

Yours truly,
Oliver Johnson

Auburn Theol. Seminary
March 16, 1886
A testimonial from Professor Hopkins:

The remarkable person who is the subject of the following sketch has been mainly residing ever since the close of the war in the outskirts of the City of Auburn, during all which time I have been well acquainted with her. She has all the characteristics of the pure African race strongly marked upon her; though Barracoons on the Guinea coast, she derived her indomitable courage and passionate love for freedom. I know not, perhaps from the Fellatas, in whom those traits were predominant.

Harriet lives on a farm where the twelve hundred dollars given to her by Mrs. Bradford from the proceeds of the first edition of this little book enabled her to redeem from a mortgage held by the late Secretary Seward.

Her household will likely consist of several old black people, "bad with rheumatism," some forlorn wandering woman, and a couple of small images of God cut in ebony. The Lord best knows how she manages to feed and clothe herself and them. She has too much pride and too much faith to beg. She takes thankfully, but without any great effusiveness of gratitude, whatever God's messengers bring her.

I have never heard that she lacked. There are some good people in various parts of the country, into whose hearts God sends the thought, from time to time, that Harriet may be at the bottom of the flour sack or of the potatoes and the "help in time of need" comes to her.

Harriet's simplicity and ignorance have, in some cases, been imposed very signally in one instance in Auburn a few years ago. Still, nobody who knows her has the slightest doubt of her perfect integrity.

The following sketch taken by Mrs. Bradford, chiefly from Harriet's recollections, which are wonderfully distinct and minute but also from other corroborative sources, gives an imperfect account of what this woman has been.

Her color and the humble condition in which she was born reared have doomed her to obscurity, but a more heroic soul did not breathe in Judith's bosom or Jeanne D'Arc.

No fear of the lash, the bloodhound, or the fiery stake could divert her from her self-imposed task of leading as many as possible of her people "from the land of Egypt, from the house of bondage."

The book is good literature for the black or white race. Though no similar conditions may arise to test the possibilities that are in any of them, the example of this poor slave woman may well stand out before them and before all people, black or white, to show what a lofty and martyr spirit may accomplish, struggling against overwhelming obstacles.

Letter from Frederick Douglass, which appeared in the first and second biography by Sarah Bradford:

Rochester, August 29, 1868
Dear Harriet,

I am glad to know that a kind lady has written the story of your eventful life and that the same is soon to be published. You ask for what you do not need when you call upon me for a word of commendation. I need such words from you far more than you can need them from me, primarily where your superior labors and devotion to the cause of the lately enslaved of our land are known as I know them. The difference between us is very marked. Most of what I have done and suffered in the service of our cause has been in public, and I have received much encouragement every step of the way. You, on the other hand, have labored privately. I have wrought in the day—you in the night. I have had the applause of the crowd and satisfaction that comes of being approved by the multitude. At the same time, the most that you have done has been witnessed by a few trembling, scarred, and foot-sore bondmen and women, whom you have led out of the house of bondage, and whose heartfelt "God bless you" has been your only reward. The midnight sky and silent stars have been the witnesses of your devotion to freedom and of your heroism. Excepting John Brown—of sacred memory—I know of no one who has willingly encountered more perils and hardships to serve our enslaved people than you have. Much that you have done would seem improbable to those who do not know you as I know you. It is to me a great pleasure and a great privilege to bear testimony to your character and your works and to say to those to whom you may come, that I regard you in every way truthful and trustworthy.

Your friend,

Frederick Douglass

Extracts from a letter written by Mr. Sanborn, secretary of the Massachusetts Board of State Charities:

My Dear Madame:

Mr. Phillips has sent me your note, asking for reminiscences of Harriet Tubman, and testimonials to her extraordinary story, which all her New England friends will, I am sure, be glad to furnish.

I never had reason to doubt the truth of what Harriet said regarding her own career, for I found her singularly truthful. Her imagination is warm and rich, and there is a whole region of the marvelous in her nature, which has manifested itself at times remarkably. Her dreams and visions, misgivings, and forewarnings, ought not to be omitted in any life of her, particularly those relating to John Brown.

She was in his confidence in 1858–9, and he had a great regard for her, which he often expressed to me. She aided him in his plans and expected to do so still further when his career was closed by that incredible campaign in Virginia. The first time she came to my house in Concord after that tragedy, she was shown into a room in the evening where Brackett's bust of John Brown was standing. The sight of it, which was new to her, threw her into a sort of ecstasy of sorrow and admiration, and she went on in her rhapsodical way to pronounce his apotheosis.

She has often been in Concord, where she resided at the houses of Emerson, Alcott, the Whitneys, the Brooks family, Mrs. Horace Mann, and other well-known persons. They all admired and respected her, and nobody doubted the reality of her adventures. She was too honest a person to be suspected. In 1862, I think it was, she went from Boston to Port Royal, under the advice and encouragement of Mr. Garrison, Governor Andrew, Dr. Howe, and other leading people. Her career in South Carolina is well known to some of our officers, and I think to Colonel Higginson, now of Newport, R. I., and Colonel James Montgomery, of Kansas, to both of whom she was helpful as a spy and guide, if I mistake not. I regard her as, overall, the most extraordinary person of her race I have ever met. She is a negro of pure, or almost pure blood, can neither read nor write, and has the characteristics of her race and condition. But she has done what can scarcely be credited on the best authority, and she has accomplished her purposes with a coolness, foresight, patience, and wisdom, which in a white man would have raised him to the highest pitch of reputation.

I am, dear Madame, very truly your servant,
F. B. Sanborn

Letter from Honorable William H. Seward:

Washington, July 25, 1868
Maj.-Gen. Hunter—
My Dear Sir:
Harriet Tubman, a colored woman, has been nursing our soldiers during nearly all the war. She believes she a claim for faithful services to command in South Carolina with which you are connected, and she thinks that you would be disposed to see her claim justly settled.

I have known her long, and a nobler, higher spirit, or a truer, seldom dwells in the human form. I commend her, therefore, to your kind and best attentions.

Faithfully your friend,

William H. Seward

While the interview process with Sarah continued, Harriet had to place her suffragette speeches on temporary hold. Although she viewed it as crucial work, she had to prioritize raising the necessary funds to carry on daily life.

Harriet and Sarah had become very close friends when Sarah had moved, years earlier, from her Geneva home in New York to nearby Auburn, New York, where her brother Samuel Hopkins was a professor of Ecclesiastical Studies at Auburn Seminary. As Sarah's husband had abandoned her and her six children, residence in Auburn was a natural fit for her. Having an established friendship with Harriet that spanned numerous years, work on the first and second biographies was also a logical progression.

Sarah's brother, the Reverend Dr. Samuel Hopkins, had been instrumental in founding the Central Presbyterian Church in 1861, after breaking away from the Second Presbyterian Church in Auburn for their refusal to support abolition. Sarah had been a Sunday school teacher of Harriet's parents, along with many others in the community. It was also the same church where Harriet and Nelson had been married several years earlier.

Sarah and Harriet's past was a bond that had brought them together, both having been abandoned by their husbands, who later died. Two of Sarah's sons had fought in the Civil War. Unfortunately, two of Sarah's sons had perished, leaving her one son and three daughters to raise on her own. Both women were mothers (although Harriet had adopted Gertie). They were also close in age, which made it easier for them to relate to one another.

Sarah brought a wealth of experience as a previously published author and close friend of Harriet. Not only had she published an earlier biography with Harriet, but she was also a well-known children's and adult author in the fiction and nonfiction genres as the sole supporter of her family. In conjunction with her professional writing, Sarah also operated a private school in her home for young ladies and girls, offering them music, writing, and mathematics lessons.

As anxious as Harriet was to return to the speaking circuit, it was equally vital for her to finish the interview process with Sarah. Both were a means of income for Harriet, and interviews were less physically taxing as no travel was involved and she could be home with Gertie and Nelson. Either way, financial security remained a constant struggle. But Harriet was not one to give up, as there was always a solution around the next corner if she kept moving forward; her faith had taught her that lesson years earlier.

While working with Sarah, a thought popped up in Harriet's mind about a potential new endeavor: her dream of opening a nursing home. Her mother's death had devastated her and left her wondering what would have happened if she had been unable to care for her in her declining years. How many other older adults in her community were alone and without care? She and Sojourner Truth had discussed this some time ago and agreed there was a significant need for it. Harriet was keenly aware of the need for a home for older people and desperately wanted one on her land. Someday, she hoped to make this dream come true by earning enough money from book sales and speeches.

28

SECOND BIOGRAPHY RELEASED

Harriet, the Moses of Her People by Sarah Hopkins Bradford, with Harriet's active participation, was released in October 1886. It brought in roughly $1,200, which Harriet desperately needed. Sarah refused to take one penny of it. Instead, she returned to teaching jobs, writing, and her family's care. Sarah was content to help her friend once again. The earnings allowed Harriet to carry on with her speaking engagements in and around Boston, although her age—mid-sixties—was starting to slow her down. According to family sources, Harriet and Sarah unintentionally omitted portions of later personal history in the revised biography due to the combination of Harriet's age, the lingering effects of the ever-present head injury, and the general lack of health care available at the time, especially to Black people.

The additional income from increasing book sales eased the pressure on Harriet and Nelson. It freed her to return to the speaking circuit on occasion, when her ongoing health issues allowed. Around the time *Harriet, the Moses of Her People* was published, Harriet went to Boston to sit for a portrait. The Boston-based *Woman's Journal*—the most widely recognized and prestigious suffrage journal in the United States—was helping promote the much-anticipated second edition of her biography.

Once again, Harriet was warmly welcomed into private homes to reduce her hotel costs in Boston and elsewhere. With the release of her revised biography, the demand to hear her in person had once again risen, and Harriet was enthusiastic about retelling her personal story and truth. She was often asked how she could have made so many harrowing trips during the harsh winters. Her response was always the same; she knew she was being guided and cared for throughout each journey—she had complete faith in God.

She often described her fellow passengers as tired, cold, wet, and hungry. Somehow, she encouraged them to keep going. She also told audiences that they often depended upon the kindness of many White people to survive their travels. Harriet spoke fondly of Thomas Garrett in particular, who had passed away in 1871. She told her rapt listeners how Thomas, who owned a shoe company in Delaware, would provide each of them with a brand-new pair of shoes and warm clothing, coats included, which most of them had never had before. His generosity inspired them to trudge on through the frozen mud or snow or, if necessary, to huddle while hiding from bounty hunters and their bloodhounds. He was emblematic of how people could treat one another, regardless of color, in the Promised Land.

Harriet's audiences always listened carefully whenever she spoke of her tenaciousness in encouraging others to "keep going" as they journeyed well over one hundred miles on foot to Philadelphia. Other Railroad stops were even farther; sometimes, if they were fortunate, they could travel by horse-drawn wagons, generously donated by numbers of conductors, en route to New York and then onward to St. Catherines, Canada, their ultimate destination.

Harriet's talks always integrated the importance of equal rights for all, most notably the ability to earn wages and vote. It would be a fiery topic for some time as she and other suffragettes—Elizabeth Cady Stanton and Susan B. Anthony—traveled separately or in small groups on the New England speaking circuit. To bring about necessary change, it was vital to talk about what her people had suffered and the rights they deserved. And to further her point, there was never any disagreement among any group, Black or White, regarding the amount of honor and courage the Black regiments had displayed fighting during the Civil War.

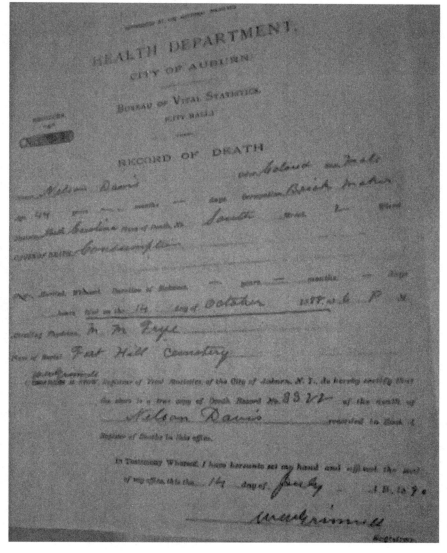

Nelson Davis's death certificate

Despite her success as an orator, things were about to take a tragic turn for Harriet at home. It remains unknown if she was away when Nelson initially became ill with tuberculosis or how long he struggled against the feared ailment. There was no cure for the disease in the latter part of the nineteenth century so, at most, the focus was on making the patient as comfortable as possible, even when it involved the nonstop coughing up of blood. Nelson passed away from the terrible disease on October 18, 1888, after nineteen years of marriage to Harriet. It was another in a series of devastating losses for Harriet, and she found solace in her work and continued to devote her time and energy to the women's suffragette movement.

29

WIDOW YEARS

Having suffered the loss of her husband, Harriet reapplied for a military pension. This time, she filled out the paperwork as a Civil War widow, using her full married name, Harriet Tubman Davis. Once again, her request was met with a deafening silence.

She had political friends remaining in government, but it seemed as if her applications were stuck in an endless realm of bureaucratic red tape. Several high-level supporters, such as Onim and Elsie McCarthy and congressmen Sereno Payne (formerly the chairman of the Merchant Marine and Fisheries Committee) and General Clinton MacDougal, wrote letters on her behalf to carry on the fight and provide her with some necessary hope.

It took two years, but Harriet finally received approval for a monthly widow's pension of $8. It was the first time in her life that she had a reliable, steady income from any source. Patience had begun to pay off for an impoverished, aging Harriet as she entered her seventies, with her health beginning to decline. While her income from the combined pension and earnings from book sales and speeches was more than she had made in her entire life and sufficient to stay afloat, the financial total was still meager. Over the years, she continued to petition for increases to her pension. Through it all, Harriet remained grateful to everyone who had helped her and was determined to demonstrate her appreciation by persevering.

30

CONVENTIONS

In July 1896, although Harriet was beginning to exhibit signs of physical frailty outwardly, her presence was requested at the founding conference of the National Association of Colored Women in Washington by Mary Church Terrell, the organization's first elected president. Harriet was among the founding members, along with Frances E. W. Harper and Ida B. Wells. Mary acknowledged that Harriet was not feeling well but, without imposing, wanted her to deliver a speech at the inaugural convention, to which Harriet agreed.

Mary Terrell had been born to enslaved parents and was one of the first African American women to have not only a college degree but a master's as well. Her father, Robert Reed Church, was a successful businessman who became one of the South's first millionaires. She married an attorney who became the first African American judge in Washington, DC. Mary immediately jumped into activism, making it central to her life's work and focusing on women's right to vote. She discovered a reluctance to extending the right to vote to African American women. She accepted it as a challenge to fight even harder for enfranchisement of all women, regardless of color.

Frances E. W. Harper was a poet, author, lecturer, and the first African American woman to publish a short story. She was born to free

African American parents in Maryland and, unfortunately, was orphaned by the age of three and raised by her abolitionist aunt and uncle, who immersed her in the movement. Following a teaching stint in Ohio, while she was in her twenties, Frances moved in with the well-known abolitionists William and Leticia Still, deepening her connection to activism. Frances eventually met Frederick Douglass and fought, along with Elizabeth Cady Stanton and Harriet, for including both women's and men's right to vote in the Fifteenth Amendment. She was married for four years, until the death of her husband, Fenton Harper, leaving her to raise her daughter by herself. Frances was named vice president of the National Association of Colored Women.

Ida B. Wells was born into slavery during the Civil War, in Mississippi, in 1862. Once the war concluded, her parents became heavily involved in the Reconstruction period's politics, directly influencing her. They also instilled the importance of education, enabling her to complete her lower-level studies and earn acceptance into Lemoyne-Owen College in Memphis. Unfortunately, she became involved in a dispute with the university president and was summarily expelled. When her parents died of yellow fever, young Ida was forced to raise her siblings. This did not deter her from becoming an educator, however.

After one of Ida's close friends was lynched, she turned to writing several exposés about the horrors of the lynchings of Black men. A backlash of threats and the burning of her printing presses forced her to move from Memphis to Chicago to avoid further acts of hostility. What Ida could not have known—nor could anyone have fathomed—was that it would take approximately 126 years for an anti-lynching law to be passed. In 1895, Ida married a famed African American lawyer, Ferdinand Barnett, and they had four children.

There were numerous reasons the National Association of Colored Women was formed, most prominently the adverse treatment of African American women, segregation, the inability to vote, and the desire to uplift the colored race. The founders, including Harriet, agreed that all those issues were best described by the adopted motto: "Lifting as we climb." The first platform Mary Church Terrell addressed in her opening speech at their first convention included job training, wage equity, and childcare. The aim was to improve the lives of all African Americans who were impoverished, as well as to improve everyone's health.

Harriet addressed the convention, retelling her gripping, harrowing tale of walking one hundred and forty miles from the South, which included occasionally taking out a pistol to keep frightened charges from giving away their position to bounty hunters and slave patrols. Harriet had to take extraordinary measures to save the people in her care. She was a master of disguises, enabling her to be an indispensable, successful spy for the Union Army.

Two months prior to this convention, in May 1896, the *Plessy vs. Ferguson* decision was handed down by the Supreme Court. Homer Plessy, a primarily Black man, purchased a train ticket and took a seat in a train car reserved for Whites. He refused to move to the vehicle for African Americans and was arrested. Judge John Howard Ferguson, a district court judge, said his constitutional rights had not been violated. The final decision was that it was legal to have separate but equal facilities for Blacks and Whites, granting racial segregation. The famous singular dissent came from Judge John Marshall Harlan, advancing the idea that the Constitution is color blind. *Plessy vs. Ferguson* was overturned nearly sixty years later, in 1954, by *Brown vs. Board of Education*.

The last suffragette convention Harriet could attend was in Rochester, New York, in November 1896. According to the local Auburn paper, Harriet's train to Rochester arrived late, forcing her to spend the night sleeping at the train station.

Susan B. Anthony introduced Harriet at the event. She was warmly welcomed by the crowd, possibly causing her to break out into one of her favorite songs, or spirituals, as she often referred to them: "Bound for the Promised Land," written by Samuel Stennett (1727–1795) in England.

> *I am bound for the promised land.*
> *I'm bound for the promised*

Oh, who will come and go with me
I am bound for the promised land

Harriet proceeded to give her usual talk, which, as always, left the gathering wanting more from their hero. Before leaving the stage, Harriet reminded them of one crucial, indisputable fact: "I was the conductor of The Underground Railroad for eight years, and I can say what most conductors can't say—I never ran my train off the track, and I never lost a passenger."

Another spiritual Harriet may have sung was "Swing Low, Sweet Chariot," a personal favorite of hers that was written by Wallace Willis, a Choctaw freedman, sometime after 1865. He lived in the old Indian Territory in what is now known as Choctaw County, near the county seat of Hugo, Oklahoma. He may have been inspired by the sight of the Red River, which he worked near, and the river's echoes of the biblical Jordan likely reminded him of the Jordan River.

31

QUEEN VICTORIA

In 1897, Queen Victoria celebrated her Diamond Jubilee—sixty years of sitting on the throne as the monarch of the British Empire—alongside Prince Consort Albert. The British Empire included all Canadian Territories, which, from the beginning of slavery in the United States, had welcomed all the enslaved people from the Confederacy to live and breathe free air. Though the British Empire was an active participant and beneficiary in the global slave trade for centuries, by Victoria's reign, the Canadian government encouraged all the formerly enslaved to earn wages equal to those of the White labor force and receive fair housing to own, rent, or board. Neither the queen nor her consort could assist those seeking their right to freedom. Still, they could cheer them on and serve as abolitionists from across the seas.

In 1852, Harriet Beecher Stowe's fiery novel *Uncle Tom's Cabin* was published, detailing the horrors of slavery. Stowe met Queen Victoria in 1856, presenting her with a signed copy. The book opened the queen's eyes to the brutality of slavery.

Stowe also met with President Abraham Lincoln, in 1862. Upon greeting the author, Lincoln exclaimed, "You're the little lady responsible for starting the war!"

There's no evidence that the two Harriets crossed paths. However, Stowe's writing significantly affected Tubman, enlightening those who might not have understood the depths of cruelty she had escaped from and the stories of those she had rescued.

The queen sent invitations to the leaders of nations and worldwide diplomats to celebrate her sixtieth anniversary of rule. News of Harriet's work and heroism had reached across the Atlantic, and the queen showed her admiration and respect for Harriet by extending an invitation to the sixtieth jubilee. Each attendee was to receive a commemorative medal to mark the ornate occasion.

Sadly, Harriet had to express her regrets due to her health. Queen Victoria gifted her with a unique shawl made of lace and linen, sending it along with a commemorative medal. The shawl became one of Harriet's favorite garments, and the medal was placed prominently in her home.

32

HARRIET UNDERGOES BRAIN SURGERY

By the time Harriet had reached her late seventies, her headaches had become much more severe, and sleep was more elusive than ever before. Her seizures had begun to increase as well. A local physician recommended brain surgery as a possibility to alleviate some of her symptoms and provide comfort for the remainder of her life. He was careful to point out that its success was not guaranteed. Harriet willingly took the gamble, open to anything that might take the edge off the pain she was experiencing. At the time, Massachusetts General Hospital in Boston was the only hospital that offered an intensive, invasive surgery to reduce the pressure on Harriet's brain. Harriet had such an extensive network of friends in the Boston area that she knew she could rely on any of them to house her during her recovery before she became well enough to return to Auburn.

The exact date of Harriet's procedure and the surgeon's name have been lost to history. However, we do know that Harriet's nursing experience in the Civil War influenced her decision to forgo anesthesia, as she had seen soldiers under her care die while enduring leg or arm amputations because of anesthesia. During the surgery, she bit down on a bullet to withstand the pain.

The surgery was successful in that it reduced the pressure on her brain sufficiently to take the edge off the intense pain, permitting her to resume a somewhat everyday life for a woman of her age. She could assist others with some small tasks in town or work in her garden. At last, she could fall asleep at night following a day's work. Although she was immensely grateful for the reduced level of pain and the other improvements, she unfortunately had to continue to endure headaches.

After her recovery, Harriet received good news regarding her petition to increase her pension. The HR 4982 bill proposed a substantial monthly hike from $8 to $25. Letters had been written and received on her behalf. She had patiently waited years only to be repeatedly told, "No."

On February 7, 1899, the Senate report in response to HR 4982 determined that the Committee of Pensions objected to the increase to $25. They acknowledged Harriet's service and dedication to the country as a nurse but argued that few nurses were on the pension roll at a rate higher than $12 per month. They didn't see a valid reason why Harriet Tubman should receive a pension of $25 per month, which would have opened a can of worms with pension increases. The Committee of Pensions decided to increase Harriet's widow's pension to $20 per month without considering her services to her country. The act, which Congress approved on February 28, 1899, read:

> Be it enacted by the Senate and the House of Representatives of the United States of America in Congress assembled that the Secretary of the Interior is authorized and directed to place on the pension roll, subject to the provisions and limitations of the pension laws, the name of Harriet Tubman Davis, widow of Nelson Davis, late private in Company G, Eighth United States Colored Infantry and pay her a pension at the rate of twenty dollars per month instead of what she was now receiving.

Sadly, the act failed to acknowledge or reflect Harriet's military service in the Civil War. At seventy-nine years old—after a lifetime of service—her annual pension earnings amounted to $240.

33

RETURN TO BOSTON

According to an article printed in the *Boston Herald* on May 31, 1905, Harriet Tubman made what was reported as her final visit to Boston. She attended an opening reception for the Harriet Tubman Christian Temperance Union at Parker Memorial Hall. She also visited the Harriet Tubman House on Holyoke Street, a temporary haven for young negro girls arriving in Boston from the South. It had been established and maintained by the colored citizens, with the aid and under the patronage of South End House.

Afterward, Harriet attended the Memorial Day ceremony at the Robert Gould Shaw Fifty-Fourth Massachusetts Regiment Memorial. The *Boston Globe* reported Harriet "was the central figure at the Robert G. Shaw memorial yesterday."

The article went on to say: "As she stood and gazed at the youthful features, tears came to her eyes. She turned and said to those near her, 'That looks like him the last morning I made him his last breakfast. This is the first time I have seen the monument close to it. I was here when they unveiled it, but the crowd was then so big. I went back to Auburn but decided to see it again sometime.'"

The paper further reported that Tubman stood at the memorial "bent with the weight of years" and described how she "gazed long and tenderly on the magnificent work of the sculptor and dropped a silent tear for the departed dead." While Harriet stood, she may have wondered who was left of her family and friends and those who had fought alongside her all those years for freedom. Who would pick up and carry on after she was gone?

While at the ceremony, Tubman also had the chance "to renew her acquaintance with the boys of the Fifty-Fourth that she had worked alongside during the war. While her step is feeble, she still has a vigorous appearance." When asked to pose for the *Herald* photographer, Harriet, now around eighty-three, gladly consented and placed herself so she would look at her best.

34

AME ZION CHURCH

The African Methodist Church (AME) was founded in 1796 and chartered in 1801 in Auburn, New York. It was officially founded in 1846 when Zion was added to its name. The congregation played a central role in Harriet's life, beginning when she and her parents moved from St. Catherines, Canada. While in Canada, they'd attended the AME Church in Salem, St. Catherines. Raising funds to build a church took far longer than the congregation anticipated. Until 1891, the congregation met in individual homes throughout Auburn. During the cornerstone laying, Harriet placed a coin with the profile of her close friend John Brown inside. It remains there to this day.

The African Methodist Episcopal Church was a haven for abolitionists and the freed Black community at large. Frederick Douglass gave passionate speeches from the pulpit. It was also a home for Sojourner Truth. And it was a way to foster community among those who fled enslavement from all across the South.

Harriet's family were active AME church members, even though her parents attended the Central Presbyterian Church, and she and Nelson were married there. That was years before AME had been built. With the building's completion, another one of Harriet's dreams had been fulfilled.

A significant part of Harriet's character, starting from when she was a little girl, was to help others, regardless of personal sacrifice. Her eventual vision was to establish a home for elderly Black Americans; she sought to help them live their final days with dignity and grace. There were few to no social services available for older people, so she deemed this a necessity, not a luxury. Her wish was to name the facility after her dear friend John Brown, who had sacrificed everything for his belief in ending slavery.

Twenty-five acres of the northern portion of land next to her house in Auburn became available and on the auction block. Harriet had a mindset to somehow obtain it as the site of her future nursing home. Although Harriet had no personal funds, she bid on the plot. She received the property through a mortgage, with the assistance of AME Zion Church, for $1,400. The property included two houses, barns, and several outbuildings. Today, the remaining building is the landmark Tubman Home for the Aged, indicating that her wishes to name it after John Brown were not followed.

AME Zion Church

In 1903, Harriet could not make tax payments due to financial struggles, so she was forced to deed the Tubman Home for the Aged to the African

Methodist Episcopal Zion Church. She only did so on the condition that AME would continue to sustain its operations after her passing. According to oral family history, AME charged seniors to reside there, which was expressly against Harriet's wishes.

Entrance to the Tubman Home for the Aged, renamed Harriet Tubman Home for the Elderly many years after her death, located at 180 South Street, Auburn, New York

Harriet Tubman Home for the Elderly

A Board of Trustees and a Board of Lady Managers assumed the debt on the property. The church worked to raise more money for renovations on a second house on the property for use as part of the home.

June 23, 1903: the day Harriet dreamt of had finally arrived. She had fought long and hard for the opening of her Home for the Aged and Indigent Negroes. She had spent her entire life helping others, whether donating money she had earned working long hours as a domestic or providing volunteer service whenever needed. She never minded laboring if it had a meaningful end. Harriet had been passionate about assisting and saving family, strangers, and neighbors throughout her life, one of the reasons so many were drawn to her, regardless of their color. Arianna C. Sparrow, a known supporter of women's suffrage who worked for African American civil rights, once commented on Harriet Tubman's humanitarianism and generosity: "No one can give her anything, for everything she has she gives away. She is as generous as the sunshine."

Harriet's logistic planning had led to this exact moment, dating back to when she first purchased her Auburn home. Owning her piece of property had given her the ability to house her parents and adequately care for them until their lives ended. It gave them the dignity they never had as enslaved people. It also afforded Harriet enough bargaining power with AME Zion Church to purchase the land on which the Tubman Home for the Aged now stood. Harriet, a woman once enslaved, stood there realizing another dream had come to fruition following the sweat of years of hard work. It was to be the very first nursing home anywhere for aging, indigent Black people—where formerly enslaved people could meet their end with grace and respectability.

Over the years, Harriet had taken boarders into her home who could not afford to pay her. Her generosity extended to requiring that AME agree to provide health care for all residents at no charge. According to the Tubman family and other sources, AME insisted on charging all residents a housing and care fee, which became a bone of contention and stalled the opening of the residence for approximately five years. AME's position contradicted Harriet's belief that the neediest and poorest in the community should be cared for at no cost—her aim from the outset. Harriet had to approve the arrangement, or there would be no home.

Frances Jane Scroggins Brown, Underground Railroad station operator who became the Matron of the Harriet Tubman Home for the Aged

When the home finally opened, residents were required to pay $100 for their spots. AME capitulated in two areas, giving Harriet some peace of mind. The best local Auburn doctors and nurses provided necessary treatment and care once a week to those who required it at no charge. The medical hall was named after her dear friend John Brown, as a compromise. Harriet stood on the lawn wondering if John would be proud of her compromise.

35

AUBURN RESIDENT

H arriet became a resident of the home named after her far too soon for her liking. Her frailty had caught up with her in a way she could no longer ignore, bringing her life to a grinding halt. It didn't matter that Harriet insisted she had a schedule to keep; her body had other ideas and, simply put, refused to carry on with putting one foot in front of the other. Harriet was forced to admit it was time to pass the torch to others to carry the message of change. She had fulfilled her duties, and now it was her turn to rest, as tricky as it was.

Harriet Tubman in 1908

She had already suffered the losses of many beloved family members and dear friends and was alone in the world. Even Sarah Bradford, her friend, biographer, and supporter, passed away on June 25, 1912.

With all Harriet had accomplished in her life—from rescuing numerous enslaved to her service in the military—she had to rely on the kindness of her Auburn neighbors to cover her residency expenses in the home that bore her name. Her monthly pension barely dented what she owed the home in her remaining years. Harriet was destined to die as destitute as the day she was born into slavery. She may have found some comfort that her bed was in John Brown Hall, named for her beloved abolitionist friend.

Harriet received visitors when she was up to it, including her nephew William Stewart; his son Charles; and two grandnieces, Alida and Eva Stewart. Family truths that have been orally passed down through the generations tell us Harriet spent a considerable amount of time with Alida and Eva. Harriet felt she had lost precious time with her grandmother Modesty in her final moments and did not want to fail her grandnieces. Fully aware of time being short, Harriet imparted as much of her legacy as possible to the young girls, so they would pass the information on to future generations. It was Harriet's dream to continue freeing as many Israelites as her family could through whatever means possible: she knew in her heart she was leaving her dream in capable hands.

She was incredibly close to some of the AME clergy, who spent time with her as often as Harriet's energy permitted.

Harriet fought bravely against her failing health for two long years. Despite close monitoring of her care by her physicians and nurses, she contracted pneumonia sometime in late February or early March of 1913. Unfortunately, pneumonia proved to be too brutal a foe, and Harriet Tubman passed away in the home she had founded on Tuesday, March 10, 1913.

36

THE PASSING OF
AN AMERICAN ICON

When Mrs. Martha Ridgeway, a nurse of Elmira, and Dr. G. B. Mack realized Harriet's death was imminent, they apprised her of her situation. Harriet requested that her clergy friends, Reverend Charles A. Smith and Reverend E. U. A. Brooks of the AME Zion Church, be present.

Harriet also requested that her nephew William H. Stewart and his son Charles Stewart come to her bedside. Her two grandnieces, Alida Stewart and Eva Stewart, were in Washington, DC, attending the first inauguration of Woodrow Wilson and, therefore, could not return in time. Another individual, Eliza Eubanks Peterson—the national superintendent for temperance work among Black people for the Texas division of the Woman's Christian Temperance Union—had previously traveled to Auburn to seek Harriet's counsel. Eliza had been unaware of either Harriet's frailty or how close to death she was. No records exist of the exact nature of Eliza's purpose or the guidance she required from Harriet. Still, Harriet was deeply disappointed that she could not provide any direction to Eliza. She was in attendance at Harriet's final service, for which, according to the *Auburn Citizen*, Harriet had given specific directions. Harriet sang when her coughing did not prevent her from doing so. Upon receiving the sacrament from the Reverend, she lay back in bed, exhausted.

Harriet began her final words, "Give my love to all the churches," and coughed severely. Her last words came from a Bible passage she had learned from Matthew, "I go away to prepare a place for you, and where I am ye may be also." Shortly afterward, per the *Citizen*, on March 11, Harriet Tubman "lapsed into a comatose condition, and death came 8:30 last evening."

It was anticipated that the body of Harriet Tubman—a woman of immense national stature—would lie in state, and many prominent people would attend her funeral.

37

HARRIET TUBMAN'S FUNERAL

The morning following Harriet Tubman's death, several hundred local citizens of Auburn, coupled with visiting dignitaries, held a service in the Tubman Home for the Aged and Indigent Negroes. Afterward, in the afternoon, Harriet's body was moved to the AME Zion Church on Parker Street. Harriet lay in an open casket from noon until 3:00 P.M. At the same time, roughly one thousand mourners paid their respects to their fallen heroine. Her body was dressed in a black dress and waistcoat, the origins of which family members were unable to verify. However, according to family history, the medal gifted to her by Queen Victoria of England was possibly pinned to her coat. Harriet's casket was draped with the American flag. The lady managers of the Tubman Home acted as Harriet's "guard of honor" during visitation. A delegation from the Charles H. Stewart post of local Union Army veterans arrived in a group, like the military honors of today.

Harriet Tubman's death certificate

For the service, approximately five hundred people managed to squeeze inside the church to listen to several eulogies. The others had to linger outside. Below are sections from a few of the eulogies:

Bishop George Lincoln Blackwell of Philadelphia:

> "If we could grow a race of Harriet Tubman, the future of our people would be secure. The battle she fought for freedom

will continue. She sought freedom, physical, intellectual, and moral."

Reverend C. A. Smith (met Harriet Tubman while serving as a Union soldier):

"My mother is gone. I learned to call her mother on the battlefields in Maryland and Virginia. I will feel eternally lonesome."

John F. Jaeckel, president of the Auburn Common Council:

"I may say that I have known 'Aunt Harriet' my whole life. The boys of my time always regarded her as a supernatural being; our youthful imaginations were fired by the tales we had heard of her adventures, and we stood in great awe of her."

Bishop J. C. Roberts of Binghamton, New York, gave the briefest eulogy of all:

"The world was to be thankful that God had spared Tubman to the world for as long as he had."

Geraldine Copes Daniels and Pauline Copes Johnson at
Harriet Tubman's gravesite in Auburn, New York

Harriet Tubman's casket was taken by horse-drawn carriage to her final resting place—Fort Hill Cemetery, Auburn, New York, as funeral attendees walked alongside. It was years later, in 1937, that a simple headstone was placed on Harriet's gravesite beneath a large tree, with two small bushes on either side, by the Empire State Federation of Women's Clubs. It stands approximately three feet high and has her name, Harriet Tubman Davis, carved on one side. On the other side, it reads:

To the Memory of Harriet Tubman Davis
Heroine of the Underground Railroad
Nurse and Scout in the Civil War
Born about 1820 in Maryland
Died March 10, 1913, at Auburn, NY
"Servant of God, Well Done"
Erected by the
Empire State Federation of Women's Clubs
July 5, 1937

38

WORLD WAR II NAVAL SHIP NAMING

H aving one's name given to a United States Naval ship is the highest honor the Navy can bestow upon the legacy of a deceased person and their family. It is generally reserved for those who have served the United States in some capacity, whether as a senior-ranking military service member or a high-level politician, such as a former president of the United States. Harriet Tubman was neither a politician nor considered a conscripted, paid member of the Union Army. Still, she had been assigned to covert spy operations by both General Hunter and General Montgomery in leading one of the most successful raids of the Civil War—that of the Combahee River, on June 2, 1863. If not for her heroism in the days leading up to the raid and the actual raid, the war's course may have changed dramatically. Due to Harriet's depth of courage under fire from the Confederate guns, the Union Army ships successfully turned off a vital shipping lane, disrupting the flow of food and armament supplies from the Deep South.

The SS *Harriet Tubman* was built by the South Portland Shipbuilding Corporation, Maine, in April 1944 and launched on June 3, 1944. It was a 441-foot long Liberty class ship. Many vessels were built to carry cargo and captured troops, and they had to be transported overseas. The ships were typically outfitted with one stern-mounted gun. Her top speed was eleven knots, equivalent to thirteen miles per hour, and she could carry 9,140 tons of cargo.

During the latter part of World War II and into the 1950s, asbestos was a common building material in homes and shipbuilding. The material was innately heat-resistant and prevented fires, which was crucial aboard any ship. No one in any US shipyard, coast to coast, could have foreseen or calculated the health risk this would inflict upon military servicemen, servicewomen, and shipbuilders over the decades that followed.

Years later, following the discovery of the direct link between cancer and asbestos exposure among those who had served aboard Liberty ships, several vessels were scrapped, including the USNS *Harriet Tubman* in 1972.

39

HARRIET TUBMAN
TUGBOAT NAMING

T he year 2022 marked the bicentennial anniversary of Harriet Tubman's birth, even though no records were kept of slave births. It's an anniversary accepted by her descendants and one of many celebrations in New York along the Erie Canal. Throughout her life, Harriet used waterways to guide the enslaved to safety, often with the support of like-minded riverboat captains. She made several trips along the Erie Canal corridor. The Erie, Champlain, Oswego, and Cayuga-Seneca Canals were all part of the Underground Railroad, which Harriet Tubman traversed on her route to Canada.

Geraldine Howard, Rita's sister, stands in front of the Harriet Tubman tugboat

On October 4, 2022, Governor Kathy Hochul of the State of New York, surrounded by several dignitaries, including Rita's sister, Geraldine Howard, named a Canal Corporation vessel after Harriet Tubman. It was a previously unnamed push tugboat on the Genesee River, a spur of the Erie Canal in Rochester. The location is most fitting, as it was a waterway Harriet used. It's also situated near Auburn, where she lived and traveled from to keep up her fight for equality, and where her final resting place is.

40

USNS *HARRIET TUBMAN*— SECOND NAVAL SHIP NAMING

Many US Naval ships have been lost at sea during wartime or scrapped in later years for a variety of reasons. As previously mentioned, the first SS *Harriet Tubman* was scrapped due to the discovery of the deadly effects of asbestos on humans. It is rare for the US Navy to reuse a ship name after the boat has gone to the boneyard. Occasionally, retired ships become floating museums if they're not junked, used for target practice, or sunk.

Recently, it was announced that Harriet Tubman will become the recipient of a second US Naval ship named in her honor. She will formally be acknowledged as the first African American woman to serve in the US military, specifically the Civil War. The USNS *Harriet Tubman* is the ninth ship in the John Lewis class, named for civil rights leader and congressman John Lewis of Georgia. One of Harriet's friends and a fellow abolitionist, Sojourner Truth, is honored in the same fleet as Earl Warren, Harvey Milk, Robert F. Kennedy, Ruth Bader Ginsburg, Lucy Stone, and Thurgood Marshall.

General Dynamics builds all the ships on the San Diego Bay. The historic shipyard will begin constructing the 742-foot-long USNS *Harriet Tubman* in late 2025. The function of the John Lewis fleet is to supply fuel to the Navy's operating carrier strike force and carry supplies. The ships can carry 162,000 barrels of oil and dry cargo.

41

HARRIET TUBMAN CIA STATUE

Numerous statues, schools, and highways throughout the country have been named after Harriet Tubman; the most prominent is the statue at the entrance to the CIA, erected on September 27, 2022. The suggestion for her statue originated with CIA officers who had studied Harriet Tubman in a leadership class, and it included details of her exploits spying and scouting for the Union Army. Harriet Tubman will always be held in the highest regard by our country's leading intelligence agency for her innate ability to go behind enemy lines with a singular goal: to save lives.

It was mutually agreed upon that the statue would reflect the agency's recent advances in diversity hiring practices. The hiring of minorities had risen to 30 percent in recent years, just before the agents requested the statue.

Robert Hanlon designed the work as a replica of the same bronze statue in Auburn, New York. The artist's rendering depicts young Harriet in bronze, holding a lantern with a pistol in her belt.

Life-sized statue of Harriet Tubman inside   Harriet Tubman statue in Harlem
the Maryland State House in Annapolis

Traveling statue of Harriet Tubman when it was in Philadelphia

Magnificent sculpture by Ed Dwight installed in June 2024 in Beaufort, South Carolina. Photo by Gary M. Krebs.

42

COMMEMORATIVE COINS

A t the time of this book's publication, a significant change is on the horizon for the twenty-dollar bill. The face of Harriet Tubman, a prominent figure and icon in American history, is set to replace that of Andrew Jackson. While this change has yet to be officially announced with written legislation in place, we can anticipate the introduction of this new currency by 2025.

While we anticipate the arrival of the Harriet Tubman twenty-dollar bill, we can delve into the unique symbolism of the commemorative coins that are currently in circulation. These coins, introduced by Representative Gregory W. Meeks, a Democrat from New York, during Black History Month in February 2020, carry a rich tapestry of symbolic meanings that reflect the legacy and values of Harriet Tubman.

In honor of Harriet Tubman, there is a gold five-dollar coin, a silver dollar, and a half-dollar coin, all marking the bicentennial of her birth. The five-dollar coin, bearing a post–Civil War portrait of Harriet Tubman, is adorned with seven of her core values on the reverse: faith, freedom, family, community, self-determination, social justice, and equality. The one-dollar coin depicts Harriet Tubman extending her hand, symbol-izing her unwavering commitment to helping others. The half-dollar coin pays tribute to Harriet as a spy, scout, and nurse. The obverse side shows Harriet holding a spyglass in front of a row of Civil War–era tents, a powerful symbol of her pivotal role as a scout and spy for the Union Army during the Civil War.

43

ELDERS HONORED IN GHANA

I n 2005, three great-great-grandnieces of Harriet Tubman, Geraldine Copes Daniels, Pauline Copes Johnson, and Laberta Gaskin Greenlea, had the distinct honor of traveling to Accra, Ghana, the ancestral homeland of Harriet Tubman. The goal of the long-planned trip was to honor Harriet Tubman for her iconic achievements during her lifetime in a manner that had never been done in her Ashanti homeland, Ghana. One of the primary intentions of the visit was to celebrate Harriet's ancestral Ashanti heritage in Ghana through her grandmother, Modesty.

Of course, many significant tributes had previously occurred elsewhere. In 2000, Governor George Pataki of New York established March 10 as "Harriet Tubman Day" to commemorate Harriet Tubman, an honor short of an official state holiday. Several states, including Maryland, also pay tribute to Harriet Tubman Day.

The tribute in Ghana was something uniquely special, starting with the sponsors. The sisters' trip was made possible due to the generosity of several groups, including Ancestral Promotions in Brooklyn; the African Poetry Theatre, Jamaica, New York; and individual residents of Auburn, New York.

Proclamation of Harriet Tubman Day

The trip included a festival, a statue dedication, a street renaming in the capital, and the enstoolment of the eldest sister, Pauline Copes Johnson. The official host of the Nana Tubman Honor was one of Ghana's first female Chiefs, a contemporary great, Nana Osei Boakye Yiadom II, who welcomed the descendants and visitors, with her entourage of Queen Mothers from various regions of the country, to a historic Nana Tubman Honor ceremony and festival. It later included an audience for the three family members with Bantamahene Nana Baffour Asare Owusu Amankwatia V, a prominent member of Asante royalty in Kumasi.

Ghanaian sculptor Opoku Biney created the statue of Harriet Tubman (Nana Tubman) depicting two liberated children with broken chains standing on either side of Harriet Tubman, and it was installed in the botanical gardens in Aburi, Ghana.

A street was named after Harriet Tubman in the compound of Nana Osei Boakye Yiadom II. On the way to the gardens in Accra, they also passed a girls' secondary school.

The most incredible honor bestowed on a living person was the enstoolment of Pauline Copes Johnson, the elder of the two sisters and direct descendant of Harriet Tubman. In the Ashanti tradition, being enstooled is traditionally reserved for the eldest. Pauline Copes Johnson previously worked at the Harriet Tubman Home, where she guided tourists around the home and shared her aunt's history with them. On the trip, she hoped to learn more about her aunt Harriet so that she could put any questions regarding Harriet's accomplishments to rest.

Statue of Harriet Tubman and two children in Ghana

Geraldine Daniels, Laberta Gaskin-Greelea, and Pauline Copes Johnson with the statue in Ghana. Behind them are Elizabeth Rankin Fulcher of the Black Women's Leadership Caucus and John Watusi Branch, Director.

The Golden Stool, or its full title, Sika Dwa Kofi, has symbolized power in the Ashanti Kingdom since the seventeenth century. Per oral tradition, Okomfo Anokye, a High Priest and one of two founders of the Ashanti Confederacy, conceived the tradition.

The Golden Stool is made of gold and stands eighteen inches high, twenty-four inches long, and twelve inches wide. Initially, it was never permitted to touch the ground and was thought so sacred that no one was allowed to sit upon it. It is decorated with golden bells and appears to have descended from the sky, landing at the feet of Osei Tutu I, the Ashanti's first king, or Asantehene. Since Osei Tutu I, the Ashanti have believed that the Golden Stool houses the very soul of the Ashanti Kingdom. It is regarded as their most prized possession. Ghanaian stools also represent a contract connecting chiefs and queens to their clans.

Gold was an integral component of Ashanti art and beliefs and was considered an earthly counterpart to the sun. It was thought to be the physical manifestation of the soul of life and, as a result, was a central component of the ruler's regalia, representing his strength and purity. The amount of gold in the kingdom represented their dominance over their rivals. To this day, the king's Golden Stool represents the primary symbol of the Ashanti Kingdom. During official ceremonies, the wooden stool is displayed as a European-style chair on an elephant hide mat. It functions similarly to a national flag.

Harriet Tubman's
Journey to Peekskill
by Mary Alice Franklin

Struggle. Determination. Heroic. Perseverance. These are words that shaped a "word cloud" in sculptor Wesley Wofford's notes as he developed a concept for his Harriet Tubman statue. Wofford describes these word clouds as "empathy-building machines" that help him to answer the question "Where am I trying to take my audience emotionally?"

He explains: "As a sculptor, I'm generating these works in my studio. It's like making a child. You never really know how it's going to go once it leaves the studio."

Now the eight-foot-tall, 2,400-pound bronze statue has made its way to Westchester County. The nationally touring sculpture will be on view in Peekskill through the end of February. It is said that Peekskill is among the secret hiding spots on the Underground Railroad, along which slaves traveled as they sought freedom. Harriet Tubman is believed to have led some of those journeys. Wofford's statue, *Harriet Tubman: The Journey to Freedom*, depicts the abolitionist leading an enslaved young girl to freedom.

Says Brian Fassett, President of the Peekskill Business Improvement District (BID)'s Board of Directors: "In light of recent events like the pandemic and the racial equality movement, the presence of this statue in our downtown takes on even more meaning...celebrating our community's rich history and cultural diversity."

Wofford explains that, although the work "seems reactionary" to the current national discussions of social justice, it was actually commissioned by a private client in 2018. "The fact that it happened to land when all of these social justice conversations started to happen was serendipitous... and illustrates that there is

Article celebrating Harriet Tubman Day—March 10, 2004

The history of the Golden Stool is a captivating tale. Before embarking on war, the chiefs sought its counsel. As the Ashanti triumphed in battles, the Golden Stool's significance grew, and their kingdom evolved into an empire.

In a misguided move, the British sought to wage war with the Ashanti in the late 1800s, aiming to capture the Golden Stool. After significant losses of soldiers on both sides, and the failure to locate the Golden Stool, the British conceded defeat and pledged to never interfere with it again. The Golden Stool continues to play a pivotal role in the crowning of Ashanti royalty and the enstoolment of other leaders, signifying clan leadership. Today, the original Golden Stool is housed in the royal palace in Kumasi, Ghana.

Enstoolment of Pauline Copes Johnson

During the enstoolment of Nana Moses (Pauline), her relatives were present, as were other dignitaries who traveled throughout Ghana to bear witness to the grand occasion. The wooden stool with the elephant hide was used for the ceremony, which began with drumming and the simultaneous pouring of a libation—most likely blessed water—by a chief into the soil. This was followed by prayers offered by the queens and the chiefs in attendance. Villagers and onlookers danced as the celebration and drumming continued. Stories were told of Harriet Tubman's heroism, of her ability to rescue those who had survived the weeks and months after being captured in the dungeons of the castles that dotted the Ghanaian shores only to be enslaved on southern plantations and their descendants. Tears were shed when Modesty's name was mentioned, reconnecting past and present and ensuring that Harriet Tubman's life and legacy would forever be cherished and honored in the hearts of the people in their original homeland.

FINAL THOUGHTS
by Jean Marie Wiesen

It has been an immense honor to collaborate in bringing newly dimensioned stories of Harriet Tubman into the world. This is a time in our country when polarized perspectives on immigration, race, economics, food security, and climate change have placed enormous pressure on all of us. Harriet was born into such a time, too, yet found herself in collaboration throughout her life, mostly while rescuing her people (the enslaved) from Egypt as instructed by God through her visions. If Harriet had not collaborated with the Quakers, her family and the countless lives that were saved would have collectively perished. She would not have risen to such heights of accomplishment if she had not trusted individuals such as William Still, Thomas Garrett, and Frederick Douglass.

Collaboration is rarely easy. Harriet had experienced so much during her enslavement that she had more than due cause not to trust anyone. Yet she saw the better angels in so many and inspired people to be stronger and more courageous than they likely ever thought they could be. I hope that this book will remind us of Harriet's great humanitarianism, self-lessness, and persistence in the face of the gravest injustices. I further hope that Harriet's work will bring people together for the necessary and worthy change that will inspire all of us to do the same. Even within the difficult work of collaboration, its inevitable setbacks and reversals, there is healing.

> "Change does not roll in on the wheels of inevitability, but comes through continuous struggle."
>
> —Martin Luther King,
> Death of Evil Sermon,
> St. John the Divine, May 17, 1956

Harriet persisted, refusing to allow her health issues to stand in the way of her mission: equal rights for her people, decent health care, and voting rights.

> "We may encounter many defeats, but we must not be defeated."
>
> —Maya Angelou,
> May 29, 2014

> "Stand for something, or you will fall for anything. Today's mighty oak is yesterday's nut that held its ground."
>
> —Rosa Parks,
> unknown date

"Don't follow the path. Go where there is no path and begin the trail. When you start a new trail equipped with courage, strength, and conviction, the only thing that can stop you is you!"

—Ruby Bridges,
September 8, 2017

"With Malice toward none, with charity for all."

—Abraham Lincoln,
Second Inaugural Address,
March 4, 1865

BIBLIOGRAPHY

"Ashanti People." Guide to Africa. Accessed February 2023. https://www
.africaguide.com/culture/tribes/ashanti.htm.

Balin, Carole. "Harriet Tubman and Sarah Hopkins Bradford: Women of
Moral Courage from Auburn's Past." Auburn Seminary. 2018. Accessed
January 2023. auburnseminary.org/voices/harriet-tubman-and-sarah
-hopking-bradford/.

Bortolot, Alexander. "Gold in Asante Courtly Arts." The Met. October 2003.
https://www.metmuseum.org/toah/hd/asan_1/hd_asan_1.htm.

Callahan, Dwight. "Why Did African Slaves Adopt the Bible?" NPR. January 24,
2007. https://www.npr.org/2007/01/24/6997059/why-did-african-slaves
-adopt-the-bible.

"Clothing and Adornment of Enslaved People in Virginia." Encyclopedia
Virginia. https://encyclopediavirginia.org/43333hpr-b5deaccd6d628b6/.

"Compensation for War Services." Harriet Tubman Historical Society.
Accessed August 29, 2024. https://www.harriet-tubman.org/compensation
-for-civil-war-services/.

Conrad, Earl. "Campaign on the Combahee." The Commonwealth, June 2, 1863.
www.harriettubman.com/tubman2.html.

———. "Charles P. Wood Manuscripts of Harriet Tubman." The Commonwealth,
July 10, 1863.

DeVan, Kathryn. "Our Most Famous Border: The Mason-Dixon Line."
Pennsylvania Center for the Book. Fall 2008. https://pabook.libraries.psu
.edu/literary-cultural-heritage-map-pa/feature-articles/our-most-famous
-border-mason-dixon-line.

Diarra, Lilian. "Ghana's Slave Castles: The Shocking Story of the Ghanaian Cape Coast." Culture Trip. January 24, 2017. https://theculturetrip.com /africa/ghana/articles/ghana-s-slave-castles-the-shocking-story-of-the -ghanaian-cape-coast.

Donnelly, Paul. "Harriet Tubman's Great Raid." *New York Times*, June 7, 2013.

Duffy, Jim. "'Now I'm Almost Home!' The Death and Funeral of Harriet Tubman, 1913." Secrets of the Eastern Shore. January 31, 2021. https ://www.secretsoftheeasternshore.com/death-of-harriet-tubman-1913/.

Ewusi, Philip. "The Golden Stool (17th c.–)." BlackPast.org. October 21, 2018. https://www.blackpast.org/global-african-history/golden-stool-17th-c/.

Explore, Beaufort. "Beaufort History: Harriet Tubman and the Combahee Ferry Raid." March 9, 2023. explorebeaufortsc.com/beaufort-history -harriet-tubman-and-the-combahee-ferry-raid/.

"Frederick Douglass Quotes." Online Library of Liberty. https://oll.libertyfund.org/.

Frederick Douglass Slaveholding Religion and Christianity of Christ. Narrative of the Life of Frederick Douglass, An American Slave, Boston: Anti-Slavery Office, 1845 Pp. 77-82 and [118]-25.

Frye, Dennis. "Purged Away with Blood: John Brown's War." American Battlefield Trust. September 23, 2009. https://www.battlefields.org/learn /articles/purged-away-blood.

Gordon, Renee. "Smooth Traveler: Devil on the Eastern Shore." *Philadelphia Sun*, April 12, 2018. philasun.com/travel/smooth-traveler-devil-on-the -eastern-shore/.

Harriet Tubman Home Historical Parks Department of the Interior. https ://www.nps.gov/places/tubmanagedhome.htm

"Harriet Tubman Is Dead." *Auburn Citizen*, March 11, 1913, http://www .harriettubman.com/memoriam2.html.

Hurlbert, Brandon. "The Slave Bible: For Slavery or Salvation?" The Torah. Accessed August 29, 2024. https://www.thetorah.com/article /the-slave-bible-for-slavery-or-salvation.

Ishak, Natasha. "Inside the Life of John Tubman, Harriet Tubman's Husband Who Didn't Follow Her North." All That's Interesting. April 1, 2023. https://allthatsinteresting.com/john-tubman.

Kates, William. "African City to Honor Tubman; City in Ghana Will Name Street, Dedicate Statue." *Star Democrat*, August 11, 2005. https://www .stardem.com/news/african-city-to-honor-tubmancity-in-ghana-will -name-street-dedicate-statue/article_c67032ed-ce41-52db-84f2 -3f95f1b742d0.html.

Keyes, Allison. "Ghana Welcomes Tubman Family Members." NPR. August 12, 2005. https://www.npr.org/2005/08/12/4797502/ghana-welcomes-tubman -family-members.

Larson, Adam. "'I Had Crossed the Line': Philadelphia, Where Harriet Tubman Found Freedom." Maryland Department of Natural Resources. May 1, 2022. https://news.maryland.gov/Dnr/2022/05/01/I-Had-Crossed -The-Line-Philadelphia-Where-Harriet-Tubman-Found-Freedom/.

Leichner, Helen. "Combahee River Raid." BlackPast.org. December 21, 2012. https://www.blackpast.org/african-american-history/combahee-river-raid -june-2-1863/.

Little, Becky. "Why Bibles Given to Slaves Omitted Most of the Old Testament." History.com. December 11, 2018. https//www.history.com /news/slave-bible-redacted-old-testament.

Mathias, Marisa. "Susan B. Anthony (1820–1906)." National Women's History Museum. https://www.womenshistory.org/education-resources /biographies/susan-b-anthony.

Myths and Facts Harriet Tubman Quotes. http://harriettubmanbiography.com /harriet-tubman-myths-and-facts.html.

Rae, Noel. "How Christian Slaveholders Used the Bible to Justify Slavery." *Time*, February 23, 2018. https://time.com/5171819/christianity-slavery -book-excerpt/.

Robbins, Gary. "San Diego's NASSCO." *San Diego Union-Tribune*, September 19, 2023. https://www.sandiegouniontribune.com/2023/09/19/san-diegos -nassco-will-build-huge-navy-ship-to-be-named-in-honor-of-abolitionist -harriet-tubman-2/.

Ryan, Orla. "Door of No Return Opens up Ghana's Slave Past." *Reuters*, August 9, 2007.

"Songs of the Underground Railroad." Harriet Tubman Historical Society. https://www.harriet-tubman.org/songs-of-the-underground-railroad/.

Stokes-Jones, Joyce, and Michele Jones-Galvin. *Beyond the Underground: Aunt Harriet, Moses of Her People*. Syracuse, NY: Sankofa Media, 2013.

"The Trans-Atlantic Slave Trade." African Passages, Lowcountry Adaptations. Lowcountry Digital History Initiative. Accessed March 29, 2024. ldhi .library.cofc.edu/exhibits/show/africanpassageslowcountryadapt /introductionatlanticworld/trans_atlantic_slave_trade.

"Underground Railroad." Quakers in the World. Accessed August 29, 2024. https://www.quakersintheworld.org/quakers-in-action/115/Underground -Railroad.

White, Jamila. "Slave Kingdoms: Episode II." PBS.org. Accessed April 11, 2024.

Wolfe, Brendan. "Slave Ships." Encyclopedia Virginia. December 7, 2020. https://encyclopediavirginia.org/entries/slave-ships-and-the-middle -passage/.

APPENDIX A

TIMELINE

HARRIET TUBMAN'S TIMELINE
1820–MARCH 10, 1913

1820   Araminta "Minty" Ross (Harriet Tubman) born in Maryland.

1827   Tubman hired out to take care of a baby at the age of six.

1834   Tubman helps a runaway slave to escape from his master—and gets hit in the head with a two-pound weight.

1844   Tubman falls in love with John Tubman and marries him.

1849   Tubman escapes to freedom and leaves her husband.

December 6, 1849   Tubman makes it to Philadelphia on foot—and becomes a free woman.

1850   Fugitive Slave Law passed

1851   Tubman returns to Maryland to help family and friends escape slavery.

1857   Tubman helps her parents escape to freedom.

1860   Tubman makes her final trip to Maryland to help others to freedom.

1861   President Lincoln issues the Emancipation Proclamation.

1861   Tubman begins her work as a nurse and teacher of former slaves for the Union Army.

1863   Tubman serves as a spy for the Union. She coordinates with former slaves from the area to gather information about the opposing Confederate forces.

June 1-2, 1863   Tubman leads an armed raid up the Combahee River in South Carolina. The mission destroys Confederate supplies and frees more than seven hundred enslaved people. Tubman is the first woman to head a military expedition in the United States.

July 1863   After the Fifty-Fourth Massachusetts Infantry, whose soldiers were African American volunteers, suffers devastating losses during a bloody battle at Fort Wagner, Tubman helps bury the dead and aids survivors.

June 1864   Tubman is granted a furlough because of exhaustion and goes to Auburn to visit her parents.

1865   Civil War ends and slavery is abolished

1865   Tubman nurses Black soldiers at Fort Monroe in Virginia. After the Civil War ends, she visits Washington, DC, and informs the surgeon general that Black soldiers are experiencing harsh conditions in military hospitals.

July 1865   Tubman asks William Seward, who is secretary of state, to help her receive payment for her work during the war. She is not successful, due in part to the turmoil of President Abraham Lincoln's assassination and

Seward's ongoing recovery from stab wounds suffered during an assassination attempt.

October 1865   Tubman is traveling home by train when a conductor orders her, using a racial slur, to go to a different car. She defends her rights but is forcibly removed.

1867   John Tubman dies in a fight.

December 1868   *Scenes in the Life of Harriet Tubman*, a biography by Sarah Bradford, is published (though the official publication date is listed as 1869). The book has multiple inaccuracies, but sales raise approximately $1,200 for a financially struggling Tubman.

March 18, 1869   Tubman weds Nelson Davis, a twenty-five-year-old former slave and Civil War veteran.

1873   Tubman is robbed by men who trick her into believing they could provide her with Confederate gold.

1874   Tubman and her husband adopt a daughter, whom they name Gertie Davis.

June 1886   Tubman buys 25 acres of land next to her home in Auburn to create a nursing home for Black Americans.

October 1886   A revised Tubman biography, *Harriet, the Moses of Her People*, is published.

October 18, 1888   Tubman's husband dies after suffering from tuberculosis.

1890s   Tubman becomes more involved in the movement for women's suffrage.

June 1890   Tubman applies for a pension as a Civil War widow.

October 16, 1895   Tubman is approved for a war widow pension of $8 a month.

July 1896   Tubman speaks at the founding conference of the National Association of Colored Women.

November 1896   Tubman is introduced by Susan B. Anthony at a suffrage convention in Rochester, New York.

1897   Queen Victoria sends Tubman a shawl and a medal in celebration of her Diamond Jubilee. The queen also invites Tubman to visit England to celebrate her birthday, but Tubman's straitened finances make this an impossibility.

Late 1890s   Tubman undergoes brain surgery at Massachusetts General Hospital in an attempt to alleviate her painful headaches.

1899   Congress raises Tubman's pension to $20 per month, but the increase is for her services as a nurse instead of her military work.

June 23, 1908   Tubman attends the opening ceremony for the Harriet Tubman Home for the Aged. It will be operated by AME Zion Church, which took over the deed to the property.

May 19, 1911   An ailing Tubman becomes a resident of the Harriet Tubman Home. Supporters raise funds to finance her care.

March 10, 1913   Tubman dies following a battle with pneumonia.

March 13, 1913   Tubman is buried with military honors.

APPENDIX B

WHO'S WHO

Last Name	First Name	Accomplishment	Birth	Death
Anthony	Susan B.	Champion of temperance, abolition, the rights of labor, and equal pay for equal work, Susan Brownell Anthony became one of the most visible leaders of the women's suffrage movement.	2/15/1820	3/13/1906
Barton	Clara	The future founder of the Red Cross was at the Battle of Fort Wagner with Harriet Tubman. She cared for the White soldiers while Harriet cared for the Black soldiers.	12/25/1821	4/12/1912
Bradford Hopkins	Sarah	The only author of Harriet Tubman's two biographies: *Scenes in the Life of Harriet Tubman* and *Harriet, the Moses of Her People*	8/20/1818	6/25/1912
Brodess	Edward	Plantation owner where Harriet was first enslaved	6/14/1801	3/9/1849
Brodess	Eliza	Wife of Edward, plantation owner	ca. 1802	ca. 1858
Brown	Frances	Matron of the Harriet Tubman Home for the Aged. She worked for Harriet in her final years.	1850	1933

Brown	John	American abolitionist and close friend of Harriet Tubman	5/9/1800	12/2/1859
Butler	General Benjamin	Commanded Fort Monroe in Virginia after the Civil War, where Harriet Tubman was temporarily stationed	11/5/1818	1/11/1893
Cannon	Patty	Illegal slave trader and serial killer when Harriet was a young child	1760 or 1769	5/11/1829
Cheney	Ednah Dow	Close friend and supporter of Harriet who lived in Boston, headed up the area's suffragette movement. Harriet often stayed with her when speaking.	6/27/1824	11/19/1904
Coffin	Levi	Abolitionist and Quaker who was actively involved with the Underground Railroad	10/28/1798	9/16/1877
Copes Daniels	Geraldine	Mother of coauthor Rita Daniels and cofounder of the Harriet Tubman Learning Center	9/25/1932	3/29/2020
Copes Johnson	Pauline	Sister to Geraldine Copes Daniels and is currently the eldest living relative of Harriet Tubman	August 1928	
Daniels	Rita	Coauthor of *Harriet Tubman: Military Spy and Tenacious Visionary* and great-great-great-grandniece of Harriet Tubman	October 1954	
Daniels Howard	Geraldine	Sister of Rita Daniels	October 1955	
Davis	Nelson	Second husband of Harriet Tubman. He escaped slavery and fought in the Civil War.	unknown	October 1888
Davis	Gertie	Adopted daughter of Harriet Tubman and second husband, Nelson Davis	unknown	unknown
Douglass	Frederick	After escaping slavery, he became one of the most powerful orators for the abolitionist cause, a dear friend of Harriet Tubman's, an ally to President Lincoln, and a famous author.	February 1818	2/20/1895

Durand	Dr. Henry K.	Hospital director at Port Royal, South Carolina. Harriet treated patients there.	unknown	unknown
Garrett	Thomas	Abolitionist and leader in the Underground Railroad movement before the Civil War. Very close ally of Harriet Tubman	8/21/1789	1/25/1871
Garrison	William Lloyd	Helped lead the successful abolitionist campaign against slavery in the United States	12/10/1805	5/24/1879
Granger	General Gordon	Led Union troops in Galveston, Texas	11/6/1821	1/10/1876
Grant	Ulysses	Eighteenth US president and commander of the Union Army in the Civil War	4/27/1822	7/23/1885
Green	Harriet	Mother of Harriet Tubman and her eight siblings	unknown	October 1880
Green	John	Purchased Modesty from the slave ship upon its arrival and gave Modesty her name. We know he forcibly fathered Modesty's child, Harriet's mother, also named Harriet.	unknown	unknown
Green	Modesty	Grandmother of Harriet Tubman. She was kidnapped from Ghana and transported via slave ship to Maryland.	unknown	unknown
Hagood	General Johnson	As retribution, he held the body of Colonel Shaw during the battle at Fort Wagner.	2/28/1828	1/4/1898
Hammond	William	Surgeon general at the end of the Civil War, whom Harriet Tubman met with on her way home	8/28/1828	1/5/1900
Hunter	General David	Union commander of the Department of the South. Harriet was assigned to him.	7/21/1802	2/2/1886
Johnson	Oliver	Abolitionist and Underground Railroad conductor	12/27/1809	12/10/1889
Lee	Colonel Robert E.	Confederate general in the Civil War	1/19/1807	10/12/1870

Lincoln	Abraham	Sixteenth US president	2/12/1809	4/15/1865
Lincoln	Mary Todd	Wife of President Abraham Lincoln. Harriet met her.	12/13/1818	7/16/1882
MacDougal	General Clinton	Later a congressman who had to approve Harriet's submitted documents for a military pension	6/14/1839	5/24/1914
Montgomery	Colonel James	Chosen by Harriet to lead the Combahee River Raid with her	12/22/1814	12/6/1871
Mott	Lucretia	Quaker abolitionist	1/3/1793	11/11/1880
Nalle	Charles	Prisoner that Harriet helped release	1821	7/13/1875
Phillips	Wendell	Abolitionist and orator	11/29/1811	2/2/1884
Ross	Ben	Father of Harriet Tubman and her eight siblings	unknown	1871
Ross	Ben	Sibling of Harriet Tubman	1823	unknown
Ross	Henry	Sibling of Harriet Tubman	1830	unknown
Ross	Linah	Sibling of Harriet Tubman	1808	unknown
Ross	Mariah	Sibling of Harriet Tubman	1811	unknown
Ross	Moses	Sibling of Harriet Tubman	1832	unknown
Ross	Rachel	Sibling of Harriet Tubman	1825	1859
Ross	Robert	Sibling of Harriet Tubman	1816	1893
Ross	Sophe	Sibling of Harriet Tubman	1813	unknown
Ross/Tubman	Araminta/Harriet		1822	3/10/1913
Sanborn	Franklin	Abolitionist and journalist	12/15/1831	2/24/1917
Seward	Frances	Wife of William and also a dear friend to Harriet Tubman	9/25/1805	6/21/1865
Seward	William	A close friend of Harriet's in Auburn, New York, and New York senator and secretary of state	5/16/1801	10/10/1872
Shaw	Colonel Robert Gould	Commander of the all-Black Fifty-Fourth Regiment during the Civil War	10/10/1837	7/18/1863
Shepherd	Heyward	He lost his life during Harpers Ferry	1825	10/17/1859
Smith	Gerrit	Abolitionist	3/6/1797	12/28/1874
Stanton	Elizabeth Cady	Along with Susan B. Anthony, Stanton fueled the movement for women's suffrage.	11/12/1815	10/26/1902
Starry	Dr. John	Heard initial shots at Harpers Ferry	1819	1899

APPENDIX C

FAMILY TREE

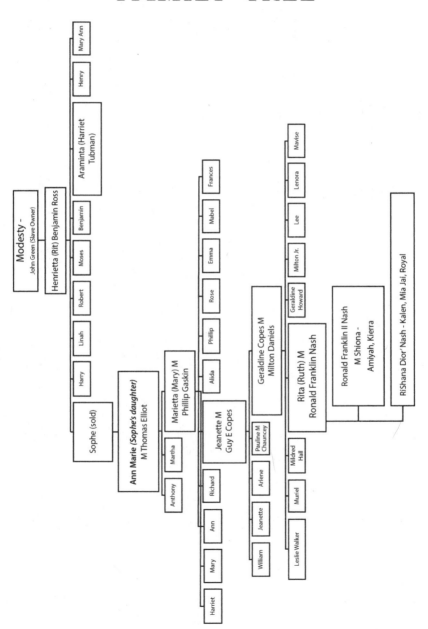

ACKNOWLEDGMENTS

This book would not have come about had I not attended the Juneteenth Celebration on the Weston, Connecticut, Green on June 19, 2022. I was unaware that Rita Daniels, a 3x great-grandniece of Harriet Tubman, was speaking. It gave me the honor of listening to Rita tell a fraction of Harriet Tubman's story and the opportunity to meet her afterward. I introduced myself as a previously published mystery crime author, enamored with history, and dubbed as an investigative author. We agreed to follow up with further conversations to see where it would take us. Rita encouraged me along the way, as the writing project unfolded, with research and oral family history that helped me to be factually accurate.

Substantial thanks go to both beta readers, Anne Skalitza (BCL) and Mariya Rivera, who meticulously read the early versions of the manuscript before it was queried out.

Major thanks go to our agent, Gary M. Krebs of GMK Writing and Editing, Inc., who has guided us through thick and thin, from our first meeting at Starbucks. I think that's where every book submission begins. Gary, you've done a fabulous job with this book, beyond anything I ever dreamed possible. I know how insanely difficult it is these days to not only find an agent but also to find a publisher. Author friends of mine continue to be self-published for that very reason and have not stopped with congratulations as a result. I am absolutely over the moon, and I know my uncle is smiling, I can feel it. So is my mom. I will probably keep thanking you forever for this opportunity.

I do have to slip in a special thanks to my cousin Mara, who assisted with the writing of the query letter. She's been like a sister to me, as has my other cousin, Annie. I'm not sure where I'd be without either of them.

I need to thank my uncle's dear friend, and mine, Claire, for reading an early version of the manuscript before he passed. It brought great joy to him to know it was nearly completed, and he learned so much more about Harriet Tubman.

Thank you, Efrem, for keeping my laptop going so I could complete it. I don't know what I would do without you.

Thank you, Rabbi Zachary Plesent of Temple Israel Westport, for your last-minute historical support.

Thank you to Lily's Market for feeding me and Sporthill Farm for the use of your loft for quiet writing when I desperately needed it.

Thank you, Queen Mother Dr. Delois Blakely, for taking time from your travel schedule to write the foreword for this important work. Your efforts in our country are crucial, coupled with what you continue to do for the African Nations, through the United Nations, as an ambassador.

Senator Blumenthal, your work for the underserved in our country does not go unnoticed, so thank you for your quote and your support.

And thank you, Pegasus, for giving us the publishing opportunity of a lifetime.

If I left anyone out, you know how to reach me.

—Jean

Thank you to my beautiful children, Ronald Franklin and RiShana Dior, for supporting me while I pursued my MBA in Education.

I want to thank my sister, Geraldine Howard, for being there for me during a time when the loss of our beloved mother during COVID-19 shattered our hearts. She is also an avid speaker on behalf of our three-times great aunt, Harriet Tubman, in Rochester, New York, and beyond.

I would also like to thank all five of my grandchildren: Kalen Nash, Kierra Nash, Amiyah Nash, Mia Jai Steele, and Royal Nash.

To my sisters and brothers, I want to acknowledge you all and let you know that I love you: Leslie Walker, Muriel Daniels, Mildred Hall, Geraldine Howard, Milton Daniels, Lee Daniels, Mavise Daniels, Lenora Swift, and Betty Jean Thompson.

Thanks to my Aunt Pauline Copes Johnson for sharing family information, traditions, and older pictures while writing this book.

Wayne Winston, you have known my mother and me for over fifteen years, and since her passing, I know she is happy that you are playing a pivotal role in managing my Harriet Tubman engagements.

Thank you, Karen Walker, Ray Bennett, RiShana Nash, Kalen Nash, Brendan Walker, Shannon Walker, and Eric Johnson, for your endless volunteer work at the Harriet Tubman Learning Center (HTLC).

I want to thank Jean Marie Wiesen, whom I met while I was in Connecticut giving a speech on my great-great-great Aunt Harriet Tubman. Jean walked up to me and offered me great kudos on my speech. She informed me that she was a writer, and we exchanged business cards. In less than a week, she called me, and we spoke about her displaying an interest in writing a book side by side on my Aunt Harriet. We agreed and moved forward with this book, and now we have coauthored this book for your reading pleasure.

I want to thank Gary M. Krebs for working diligently to get our contract with Pegasus and for pivotally liaising with Jean Marie Wiesen so that we could complete our edits on a timely basis.

I have had the pleasure to speak with Queen Mother Dr. Delois Blakely, our foreword writer, who only had rave reviews to share about the work my

Aunt Harriet accomplished during her lifetime. Queen Mother also spoke about the importance of continuing Aunt Harriet's legacy through education. She was happy I had started the Harriet Tubman Learning Center (HTLC) in her honor. The main objectives of the HTLC are to promote literacy for underprivileged youth and continue to spread Harriet Tubman's well-deserved legacy. Please donate to support the Harriet Tubman Learning Center by clicking on the QR Code below.

—Rita

https://www.harriettubmanlearningcenter.org

ABOUT THE AUTHOR:
JEAN MARIE WIESEN

Jean Marie Wiesen has been traditionally published in the mystery crime genre. She has appeared at several local book signing events and talks. She attended Art Center College of Design in Southern California, majoring in still photography and minoring in creative writing. The author continued polishing her writing craft under the tutelage of David Pollock, a local British author in Westport, Connecticut, for several years. She gleaned many of her mystery crime experiences from her eighteen years as a volunteer EMT with Westport EMS, working alongside the Westport Police Department, earning the moniker of investigative author. When not writing or plotting, Jean enjoys hiking with her dogs and sharing/learning with others interested in sharpening their writing skills.

Visit Jean Marie Wiesen at:

https://www.facebook.com/authorjeanmariewiesen/

Write to Jean Marie Wiesen at: wiesenjeanmarie@gmail.com

ABOUT THE AUTHOR: RITA DANIELS

Rita Daniels was born and raised in Auburn, New York, where Harriet Tubman spent the last fifty-two years of her life. She is one of nine siblings to Milton and Geraldine Copes Daniels and has two adult children, Ronald and RiShana, as well as five grandchildren, named Kierra, Kalen, Mia, Amiyah, and Royal.

She earned a master's degree in education and a bachelor's degree in human resources (cum laude) from Trident University International. Her tireless efforts in promoting equality, justice, and freedom have earned her love and respect from communities nationwide.

It's worth noting that Harriet Tubman, a renowned historical figure, passed away illiterate at ninety-two. Illiteracy affects many people in the United States and around the world. Rita's goal is to combat illiteracy with the help of others. Through the Harriet Tubman Learning Center (HTLC), she aims to offer educational solutions to children and communities that are struggling academically.

Rita is also an accomplished speaker who has spoken at various events. Some of the events that she has spoken at include the Black Women's March in Washington, DC; the Women Against Violence event in Washington, DC; the Juneteenth Black-tie Dinner in Bridgeport, Connecticut; and the Harriet Tubman Freedom Day event in Philadelphia, Pennsylvania. She has also spoken at the National Congress of Black Women in Washington, DC; the Association for the Study of African American Life & History in Pittsburgh, Pennsylvania; and the Black Moses Freedom Festival in Beaufort, South Carolina.

Write to Rita Daniels at daniels.rita09@gmail.com.

Learn more at https://www.harriettubmanlearningcenter.org.

INDEX